JE 3 '98

simply upholstery

simply
upholstery

BY THE EDITORS OF SUNSET BOOKS

SUNSET BOOKS INC. • MENLO PARK, CA

SUNSET BOOKS INC.

Director, Sales & Marketing: Richard A. Smeby

Editorial Director: Bob Doyle

Production Director: Lory Day

Art Director: Vasken Guiragossian

SIMPLY UPHOLSTERY was produced in conjunction with
Roundtable Press, Inc.

Directors: Marsha Melnick, Susan E. Meyer

STAFF FOR THIS BOOK:

Developmental Editor: Linda J. Selden

Senior Editor: Carol Spier

Book Design: Areta Buk/Thumb Print

Consulting Upholsterer: Jody Xuereb, J & B Decorators

Technical Writer: Zuelia Ann Hurt

Illustrations Drawn By: Phoebe Adams Gaughan; *Painted By:* Celia M. Mitchell

Photo Research: Ede Rothaus

Editorial Assistant: John Glenn

Production Coordinator: Patricia S. Williams

Cover Photograph: Philip Harvey; *Photo Direction:* JoAnn Masaoka Van Atta

Photography Acknowledgments: Pages 1–5 and all bolts of fabric: Michael Chan;
fabrics courtesy of F. Schumacher & Co. *Pages 6–7:* Eric Roth. *Page 8:* Phillip
Ennis; Designer: Mark Hampton. *Page 10:* Bradley Olman. *Page 11:* Phillip Ennis.
Page 13: John M. Hall; Designer: Sig Bergman. *Page 14:* Richard Mandelkorn;
Designer: Celeste Cooper. *Page 15, top:* Phillip Ennis; Designer: Butler's at Far
Hills. *Page 16, bottom:* John M. Hall. *Page 17:* Eric Roth; Designer: Elizabeth Klee
Speer, Inc. *Pages 112–126:* Michael Chan.

ISBN 0-376-01185-8

Library of Congress Catalog Card Number: 97-60842

Printed in the United States

For additional copies of SIMPLY UPHOLSTERY or any other *Sunset* book,
call 1-800-526-5111.

table of **contents**

be creative

YOUR FIRST THOUGHTS WHEN YOU CONSIDER reupholstering a piece of furniture are probably aesthetic—you want to give the piece a new look by replacing the cover. Maybe the old cover is worn, or maybe it simply no longer fits your decor. Your second thoughts are probably technical— upholstered furniture wears its cover like skin, and you wonder what's involved in replacing it. Soft, lovely fabric, tacks, staples, and glue seem at first to be a mixed metaphor, but as you reupholster you'll see that the aesthetic and technical go comfortably hand in hand. If you approach both aspects creatively, you'll find the entire process manageable, fun, and rewarding.

thinking creatively

OVERLEAF: Upholstering pulls the wrinkles out of casual fabrics. Here, natural linen stays fresh while ticking stripes sit tidily, enhanced by neat self-welting.
BELOW: Decorative tacks secure the fabric next to the exposed frames of the armchair and needlpoint-topped ottoman. Note the unusual back treatment on the armchair.

you are no doubt asking yourself where to begin. As with any decorating project, you begin with a vision and a plan. You'll need a clear idea of how you want your furniture to look, as well as a good understanding of the structure of the cover and the process you'll use to replace it. Most of this book is devoted to the process, but before you can start to work, you'll need new fabric. So begin by taking a good look at your furniture and your decor, and make some decisions. The answers to the following questions will help you choose well, and ensure that you're prepared.

Are you decorating or redecorating? Creating a whole new ambiance or just changing one or two pieces? Will you be integrating your reupholstery with a new or existing decor? Is the piece key to the scheme, or does it take its cue from other elements in the room?

What about style and ambiance? What style is the furniture you plan to redo? What kind and how much of a statement should your new cover make: Quiet? Breathtaking? Witty? Tailored? Casual? Have you considered the trims as well as the fabric? Is the piece in everyday use, reserved for entertaining, or more decorative than functional?

How complicated is the furniture? The simpler the shape of the piece, the easier it will be to re-cover.

What shape is your furniture in? Does it simply need a new cover, or will the reupholstery require structural repairs? This is an important question, because substantial repairs make the job much more difficult for an inexperienced hand. Before going too far, browse through Part Two, pages 18–111, to get an idea of what's involved.

Are you doing the reupholstery alone? What sort of skills do you have? Do you have a work space to devote to the task? Can you lift and turn the furniture yourself? You don't need a lot of equipment for upholstery, but a reasonably sturdy sewing machine is essential and an electric staple gun makes the work proceed efficiently. Do you have access to an upholstery-supply vendor or know an upholsterer who will sell you supplies? If you have any sewing experience, you'll find it helpful when handling the fabric.

Is the furniture worth the investment in time and money? Upholstery fabrics tend to be costly, and once you start to take apart the old upholstery, there's no turning back. New upholstery won't transform a piece of moderate quality into one of great value; you might consider slipcovering or replacing an inexpensive piece.

The preceeding questions are important because upholstery, unlike a slipcover, is integral to the furniture, and whatever fabric and color choices you make should have lasting appeal. Before you commit yourself to fabric, you should be geared up to meet the challenge ahead. So, as you consider your answers, browse through this book to see how the process works. And rest assured, reupholstery is more complex than difficult—there are lots of things to understand, but once you grasp them the work is quite logical.

There are three parts to this book. This first section discusses design, fabric, and trim. The second explains all the general techniques needed for upholstery, and walks you through the process of reupholstering a classic wing chair, with options given for handling other common types of furniture. The third presents the reupholstering of the wing chair in 50 photographs—take a look, you'll see it's not really such an intimidating process.

Jacquard weaves are always good choices for upholstery fabric. They can be dressy, *upper photo,* or casually elegant, *lower photo.* Damask is a type of Jacquard that has two usable sides; you have a choice between positive and negative color placement. With the exception of the fern pattern and the solid green rib in the lower photo, all fabrics shown are reversible.

upholstery design

at this point everything about upholstery may seem mysterious. But you can relax—other than choosing the fabric and trim, there aren't really many decisions to be made. The furniture itself dictates the basic design of the upholstery, so the construction of the cover is a given. When you remove the old fabric, you'll be mapping your route, because once the old cover is off, you simply retrace your steps to replace it.

A brushed twill stripe gives a tailored finish to this classic club chair. Note how well the pattern matches and how cleverly it miters on the ottoman top.

When you contemplate the design possibilities for your reupholstery, you will be thinking of several interdependent factors: You'll think first of the furniture—its shape and size, and its place in your decor. And you'll think about possible fabrics and the way in which their color, pattern, texture, sheen, and weight interact with the rest of your decor. The object of the design process is to devise a new cover that sits stylishly in its surroundings. Part of this process is creative and part is practical—you want to choose fabric and trim that are appropriate to the design lines of the furniture.

Begin your design process by collecting ideas. Clip pictures of similar pieces of furniture from magazines and catalogs, and collect pictures of rooms whose ambiance is appealing as well. Visit furniture stores and designer show houses if you can. Identify why certain ideas appeal to you—is it the color, the fabric, the trim details? Or is it something unconventional or especially clever about the overall design? Although you can't alter the principal lines of the furniture, you can sometimes change details, such as the proportions of a skirt, or incorporate additional trims, such as fringe or tassels. Most important, color and pattern can be used creatively—you can mix complementary patterns or use unexpected trims.

Your challenge is to embellish the cover so as to give your reupholstery a character that is traditional or unique, as you wish. Fabric can be understated, unusually colored, or importantly patterned. Embellishments might include matching or contrasting welting in the seams; flat, pleated, or gathered skirts to cover the legs; and decorative trims such as fringe and tassels. The way in which you use them—their color, material, and proportion—or your choice to omit them altogether will give your design panache. Remember that in upholstery design—as in clothing—less is often more, and simplicity can be very effective. Put the furniture's design first; your reupholstery should uphold the integrity of the piece itself.

One word of caution: Some reupholstery jobs just aren't meant for first-timers. Don't attempt to redo a chair that's already stripped down to the frame—you'll never re-create the appropriate contours. Stay away from tufted furniture—it's tricky to do, and you may have difficulty acquiring buttons with shanks strong enough to take the tension. Furniture with concave curves is difficult to cover, because there's nothing to hold the fabric flush against the curve. Large pieces aren't necessarily more difficult than small ones, just more cumbersome; and, of course, they require more fabric.

Before you finalize your design, look at samples of the new fabric and trims in the room where the furniture sits. You'll want to be sure that the colors, patterns, textures, and weights look well with your other furnishings. (If you are undertaking a major decorating or redecorating task and feel insecure about creating color schemes, you'll find many good books on the subject in the decorating and art sections of bookstores and libraries.) Look at samples in both natural and artificial light. Smooth them over your chair or sofa to get an idea of the way they'll appear once installed. If you can't borrow samples from a supplier, don't economize by skipping this step—buy a piece large enough to show how the fabric works.

The upholstery in this traditional room shows a good use of pattern. The large motif of the damask is well positioned on the easy chairs, and the bold stripe adds interest to the elegant sofa.

choosing fabric

TOP: Printed fabrics come in all manner of patterns—geometric, naturalistic, stylized, and romantic. Some even simulate woven goods such as damask.

BOTTOM: Woven plaids and stripes are available in virtually any scale and in myriad weights, textures, and finishes.

most furniture is upholstered with fabric, and fabric offers you a world of design possibilities. You may know from the outset which type of fabric you wish to use—you may even know the specific pattern. But if you don't, bear in mind that while there are times when a piece of furniture begs to be covered in a specific fabric, there are other times when a fabric can provide a piece with a new character. Be open to both possibilities. Also, read The Fabric Treatment, pages 32–35, and Measuring and Estimating, pages 36–42.

When you are designing it is important to think about the aesthetic as well as the practical characteristics of fabric. Fabric allows you to introduce pattern, color, and texture to your decor. *Pattern* may relate to or establish a style. When you think of styles such as country, lodge, French or English, Victorian or another period, distinct pattern images come to mind for each. *Color* establishes mood and can change your perception of space or proportion—and some palettes are associated with specific decorating styles. *Texture* contributes to the way fabric reflects or absorbs light, and thus affects its color. Fabrics can be smooth, soft, crisp, or coarse textured— or a combination of these. Fabrics such as bouclé, velvet, and matelassé have texture that adds dimension. The structure of a fabric's weave, the type and weight of the fiber it is made from, and the finish it is given all contribute to its texture. These latter characteristics also give each kind of fabric its *hand* (a term used to describe the way a fabric handles, or behaves, how stable it is, how well it will mold over the furniture, how bulky it is, and whether it will withstand the stress of tension and staples); they determine it's suitabity for upholstery.

Confused? Even though you may not be familiar with the jargon applied to fabrics, you can use your eyes and hands to get an idea of a fabric's suitability. Crisp fabrics do not usually mold well. Thick fabrics can be bulky and unattractive when pleated over a scroll arm or made up as welting. Sheers and soft or slippery fabrics are not usually appropriate. Loosely woven fabrics won't take the stress, but some suppliers will laminate them to a stable lining. Visit furniture stores to get a firsthand look at the way different fabrics are used, and be sure to handle a good-size sample of any fabric you contemplate using before you purchase it.

What kind of fabric should you use? For upholstery, home furnishings fabrics—often called *decorator fabrics*—are best. Not only do they offer great aesthetic options, but they've also been engineered to have a suitable hand, to wear well, and often to be stain resistant. Additionally, they're usually quite wide (54"–60") so they're more efficient to work with. Depending upon where you live, a wide selection of decorator fabrics may be available at your local fabric stores. If not, you can often order them through a furnishings store or interior designer. Home furnishings fabrics can be very costly, and upholstery can require a surprisingly large amount of yardage. If your budget is limited, don't fall in love with a fabric having a large pattern repeat that you're likely to need twice as much of as you would a solid.

When you are considering fabrics don't confuse *fiber* with *fabric*. Fiber is what fabric is made of. Fibers are either natural—cotton, linen, silk, wool—or man-made. Some man-made fibers are created from natural materials; rayon, for example, is derived from wood. Others, such as nylon, polyester, and acrylic, are true synthetics, which are often petroleum based. The way a fiber is spun, woven, and finished determines the kind of fabric it becomes. There are many, many kinds of fabric (broadcloth, velveteen, chintz, and damask, to name just a few) and many, but not all, can be made from more than one fiber.

Subtle trims put the finishing touches on these dressy pieces. On exposed-frame furniture, gimp decorates as well as conceals the fabric edge; corded medallions and tassels are quiet accents on the chaise.

Upholstery fabrics are often blends of cotton and other fibers, usually linen or rayon but sometimes silk or wool, or a synthetic such as polyester. Elegant fabrics sometimes feature metallic or Lurex threads as well. Linen, rayon, and silk all add sheen and take dye well, so fabrics made with them often appear luxurious and have especially intense colors. Cotton and wool are both durable. Cotton comes in many weaves, weights, and finishes, and it's also easy to handle. Silk comes in many weights, textures, and finishes, and the different silks have widely varying characteristics ranging from fragile to durable, and from easily handled to frustratingly slippery. Some silks water-spot easily, and a single drop of condensation from a cold glass can make them look soiled. Most silks are extremely sensitive to sunlight; they fade badly and sometimes deteriorate with constant exposure. On the whole, it is best to avoid fabrics with a high synthetic content but textile engineers are constantly improving them, so if one appeals, ask a reputable vendor about it.

choosing fabric

What about weave and finish? Upholstery fabrics should have a tight weave and they should feel stable, but not stiff, when you handle them. Fabrics with plain, twill, or Jacquard and damask (motif-patterned) weaves are common choices; satin weaves are sometimes used as well, especially as stripes. Velvets and chenilles, tapestry weaves, and some Jacquards are more difficult to work with; they're bulky and fray easily, but they're easier to use for upholstery than for sewing projects. Printed fabrics usually, but not always, have a plain or twill weave. Plain and twill weaves sometimes have a glazed finish; cotton chintz is one example. Some home furnishings fabrics are treated with a stain repellent. Medium-weight, nonpile, nonslippery fabrics are the easiest to work with.

The clean lines of these contemporary dining chairs are softened by their quilted covering. The sofa has an interesting arm treatment—plan very carefully before you attempt to emulate special details like this one.

Which fabrics will be suitable? Use those that are stable but not so stiff that they can't be stretched over the furniture. This is why it's so important to test the hand—the feel and drape—of your fabric and not to base your selection on color and pattern alone. Consider also the furniture you'll be covering and the amount of use it will get. Leathers are traditional choices for some types of furniture; novices should limit leathers to small projects. The same applies to true tapestries, such as kilims and other flat-weave rugs—they might look great when applied by a professional but would be difficult for a novice to handle on anything more complex than an ottoman top or simple drop-in chair seat. Old textiles such as quilts and coverlets are unlikely to hold up over time.

Which kind of fabric patterns are best? Whichever kind you like, but bear in mind that your upholstery skills are more critical when you work with patterns such as plaids, stripes, or midsize repeats that need careful matching. On the

other hand, patterns with large repeats are actually easier to handle because it's more important to center than match them, and plain fabrics are likely to flaunt every flaw in your work. Always consider the scale of the furniture when choosing a fabric, because a pattern that isn't in scale with the furniture might or might not be pleasing or look well in the overall decor. Whatever your inclinations, remember that the fabric makes the upholstery, and good use of a pattern will really enhance your furniture. When you put the fabric on the furniture, you'll have plenty of opportunity to adjust the fine points of the pattern match, so don't automatically shy away from a repeating design.

What about fabric quality? Be a savvy consumer. You're about to put quite a bit of work into your project, so don't consider buying fabric that has flaws in the weave, printing, or finish, or that seems in any way to be of poor quality. Purchase your fabric from a reputable vendor. Be sure the fiber content and maintenance requirements are clearly identified. Buy all of each color or pattern from one bolt because dye lots can vary.

What about cost? Reupholstery is an investment in time and materials, and wrong choices can't be easily tossed aside. So don't take the cost lightly—if you're going to spend the time and want the cover to wear well, it will be worthwhile to use the best fabric you can afford. If your budget is limited, opt for a fabric with a smaller repeat so you won't need vast amounts of it.

ABOVE: On the brilliant yellow sofa, note the use of matching and contrasting fringe, and the triple pleated skirt. The pleats on the ottoman are handsomely buttoned.
BELOW: Velvet has many incarnations. Here, from left, a bicolor cut velvet, a subtle "antique" strié, two plain velvets, and an exuberant multicolor velvet-and-rib stripe.

choosing trim

ABOVE: Tapestries and crewel will give a rich finish, and they're available in contemporary as well as traditional patterns. But think twice about choosing them if you share the furniture with a cat.

BELOW: A piece such as this simple ottoman makes a great first reupholstery project. Here a generous knotted fringe acts as a skirt.

welting, decorative cording, tassels, fringe, braid, gimp, ribbon, and even sporty rickrack—trims lend polish and panache to upholstery. In some cases you also have the option of using decorative upholstery tacks to embellish your work. Trims should usually be in scale with and have the same visual weight as the upholstery; however, there are times when larger or heavier trims are very effective. You can make welting (fabric-covered cording) from your fabric or from one that complements it. You'll find the best selection of other trims in a home furnishings fabric store.

If you like trims, you're likely to find shopping for them both exhilarating and frustrating. There are so many choices, you'll no doubt be inspired to take advantage of them. But select wisely—you may be surprised by their cost. If trim is an important part of your upholstery design, be sure you can find what you want before you purchase the fabric; you may want to adjust one or the other until you find a mix that looks great and fits your budget.

In upholstery the way in which trim is attached to the cover depends upon its placement—some is sewn on, but most is tacked in place as the cover is attached to the frame. If your furniture has welting or decorative cording inserted between the pieces, you should plan to incorporate a similar trim in the new upholstery, because it protects the edges of the cover from wear. Before committing to a trim, be sure you understand how it will be applied. Flat trims aren't suitable for inserting between pieces and, unless your

cover features a skirt, you'll have no opportunity to bind any edges. Read The Fabric Treatment, pages 32–35, and browse through Putting on the Cover, pages 77–111.

Most decorator trims are made of cotton, rayon, or a blend of the two. They come in myriad colors, but finding a perfect match for your fabric may prove challenging. Remember, a trim that makes a subtle or strong contrast can be more interesting than one that blends into its background—and you use trim to add interest anyway. When you want a perfect match, welting may be your best choice. Some vendors can arrange to have trims such as tassels made to order.

into the **workroom**

now that you've given some thought to the way your new upholstery should look, you're ready to figure out how you're going to put a new cover on your chair or sofa. As you read through the general techniques explained in the next section, remember that once you begin, your furniture will be your guide. Yes, there are many tasks involved and, yes, they all work together, so it really helps to have a good understanding of the overall process before you begin. Think of upholstery as a puzzle. If you have a logical mind, enjoy working with your hands, and pay attention to the way your work looks, you'll find the challenge easy to meet.

Be creative, be focused, be confident—let these phrases guide you through your reupholstery. If you gather ideas, assess the task ahead, and then take the time to plan your project, you should be able to follow through with flair.

A floral might not be your first thought for covering a club chair, but the scale of this graphic pattern makes the chairs look both trim and pretty.

techniques

ROLL UP YOUR SLEEVES AND GET READY TO BEGIN. In the following pages you'll learn to understand your furniture, become familiar with the tools and terms of upholstery, and see that when this complex process is broken into its component techniques, it becomes logical and manageable. Don't try to fit the techniques into a sequential plan of action—most of reupholstery doesn't work that way. As you work, you combine many actions to cut, place, fit, and attach the parts of the cover. In the chapter Putting on the Cover, you'll see how each part of the process affects the others. So read on. When you've finished these chapters, you'll be set to reupholster your first piece of furniture.

analyzing your furniture

Before you can reupholster a piece of furniture, you need a solid understanding of how it is put together: What are the hidden structural components? What are the design features that give the piece distinction? The structure and design together dictate the shape of the furniture and the nature of the upholstery. Once you understand them, you've the guidelines for the job ahead.

Begin by analyzing the piece of furniture you're about to reupholster: What do you think is going on under the cover? How is the chair built? What style is it? Does it have springs? Does it have arms, and if so, what are their style: Scroll, rolled, wing? Fully upholstered? Partially upholstered with an exposed wood frame? All wood with no fabric? Are the legs exposed or covered by a skirt? Are there cushions? Look at your chair from every angle and ask questions such as these.

You won't have all the answers until you remove the existing upholstery, but if you review the following information and compare your chair to the examples given, you should have a pretty good idea of what to expect. When you finally do get down to work, you can turn back to this chapter to better understand the things you uncover and how to deal with them.

THE FRAME

No matter what the fine points of their design are, most chairs and sofas have an inner frame built of similar structural elements. Although you can't yet see the frame of your chair, familiarize yourself early on with what are likely to be its basic parts—its bones—so that the contents of the following chapters will be meaningful to you.

A traditional wing chair has a complex frame. A chair without wings or without arms will have fewer components arranged somewhat differently from those on a wing chair, but the names of like members will remain the same. Bear in mind that rails and liners are always horizontal members; posts and slats are always vertical members.

On this wing chair the arm rail forms a horizontal scroll and the arm post forms a vertical scroll. Between them is a curved double-scroll fascia. Note that the inside of the fascia is the area adjacent to the inside arm, not the area between the two scrolls. ▽

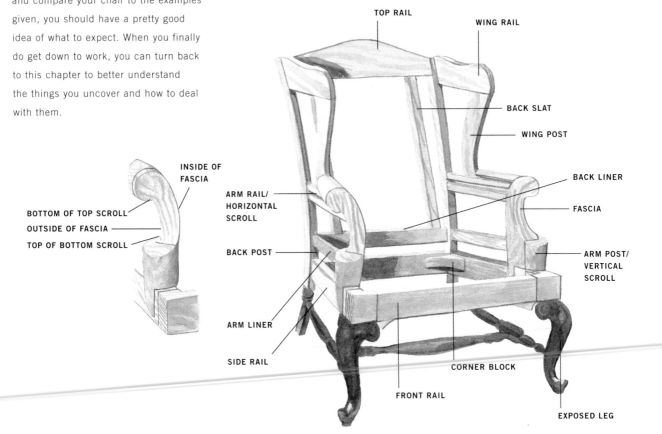

INSIDE OF FASCIA

BOTTOM OF TOP SCROLL
OUTSIDE OF FASCIA
TOP OF BOTTOM SCROLL

TOP RAIL

WING RAIL

BACK SLAT

WING POST

BACK LINER

FASCIA

ARM RAIL/
HORIZONTAL
SCROLL

BACK POST

ARM POST/
VERTICAL
SCROLL

ARM LINER

SIDE RAIL

CORNER BLOCK

FRONT RAIL

EXPOSED LEG

TIPS FROM THE PROS

✂Professional upholsterers generally replicate what they find inside a piece of furniture. If you do the same, you'll find the undertaking isn't as confusing as it may seem right now.

THE LAYERS OF MATERIALS

On top of the frame are multiple layers of materials that round out and supplement the supporting understructure. These layers are finished with a cover of decorative fabric. Depending upon the condition of your furniture, you may reuse or replace some or all of these layered materials as you reupholster.

This drawing of a wing chair shows a typical assembly of materials on a complicated piece of furniture. If your chair is of high quality, or older, it may look like this one inside. ▽

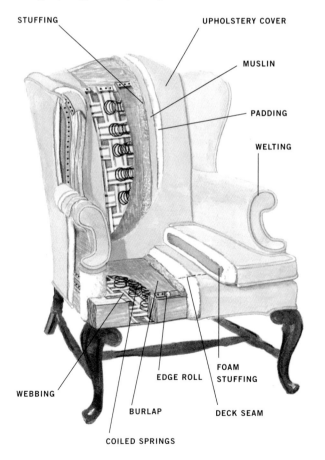

STUFFING
UPHOLSTERY COVER
MUSLIN
PADDING
WELTING
FOAM STUFFING
EDGE ROLL
DECK SEAM
WEBBING
BURLAP
COILED SPRINGS

This drawing of a platform rocker shows a typical assembly of materials on a less complicated piece of furniture. In this case the chair has zigzag springs, but it could also have the coiled variety. Note that an extra strip of padding appears in the lumbar area between the burlap and the stuffing, a frequent feature of contoured casual furniture. ▽

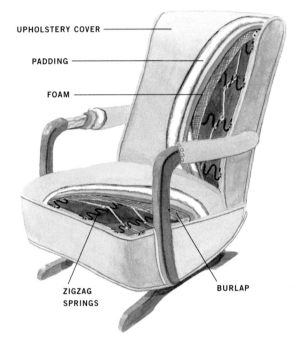

UPHOLSTERY COVER
PADDING
FOAM
ZIGZAG SPRINGS
BURLAP

This drawing of a side chair shows a typical assembly of materials on a drop-in seat—sometimes called a *pad seat* or *slip-seat*—constructed without springs. Sometimes you'll find rubberized webbing instead of the jute type; this gives some spring action and additional comfort. Redoing a drop-in seat is an excellent beginner's project. ▽

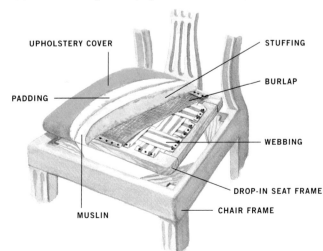

UPHOLSTERY COVER
STUFFING
BURLAP
PADDING
WEBBING
DROP-IN SEAT FRAME
CHAIR FRAME
MUSLIN

THE SEAT OR DECK CONSTRUCTION

The seat of a chair or sofa can be topped with loose cushions, in which case it's called the *deck*. The deck is usually made of two sections of fabric. The front section is called the *lip*. It usually joins to the back section of the deck just behind the front of the arms with either a straight or U-shape seam; it extends to the front edge of the furniture and wraps down to end under the front rail, as on the wing chair on the previous page, or it stops at the top edge of an attached front boxing strip or border. The back section of the deck doesn't show and can be made from a less expensive fabric than the rest of the cover.

When there are no loose cushions, one section of cover fabric is stretched from the back rail directly over the layers of padding and wrapped onto the front of the furniture. This construction is called *tight seat* or *solid seat* upholstery. The rocker on the previous page has such a seat.

The interior springs in furniture with loose seat cushions can be either attached or in a spring-edge construction. In the former, coil springs are attached within the bottom rails of the frame, or zigzag springs are attached to the tops of the bottom rails. ▽

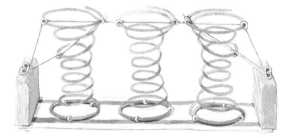

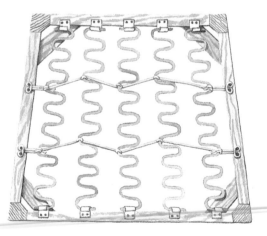

In spring-edge construction the tops of coiled springs are framed with and clamped to a wire, called an *edgewire*, which secures their configuration. The edgewire moves down with the springs as pressure is applied to the lip's front edge. ▷

FURNITURE DETAILS

The following five drawings show a variety of furniture styles with diverse construction techniques. You may identify different details from several of the drawings on your single piece of furniture.

Exposed frame construction: This chair has an exposed wood frame with an open arm. Both the back and seat are solid; that is, they are fitted tight without loose cushions. All upholstery edges are finished with a trim that is glued on. ▽

Tight seat and back construction: This traditional-style love seat has a solid seat and back. The back curves up prominently into what is often called a camelback. The scroll arms are set back from the front of the seat. ▽

Overstuffed construction: Furniture such as this club chair and matching ottoman are designed for optimal leisure-time comfort, often with puffy, overstuffed upholstery. This one looks as though it has a separate back cushion, but it really has a tight back with softly pleated, rounded corners. It has roll arms with flat fascias set back from the front of the seat and a T-shape loose seat cushion, but in many ways it's a pared down version of the spit-back sofa. ▽

Modular furniture: A modular, or sectional, sofa has multiple units that can be rearranged. Modular furniture sometimes includes a corner unit with a curved seat and contoured back; the end units are sometimes armless. This sofa has loose seat and back cushions, but some modular furniture is tightly upholstered. Upholster each section separately. ▽

Split-back construction: At first glance this couch appears to have three back cushions. In reality, it has a solid back and indentations that align with the junctions of the loose boxed seat cushions. Split backs can be curved across the top, such as this one, or straight. They can have two or three sections. This couch has scroll arms with soft, fan-shaped pleats on the fascia and a fringe-trimmed skirt with illusory pleats. ▷

recognizing design variations

In addition to the basic construction variations, there are myriad design options that give furniture its style. Here are just a few.

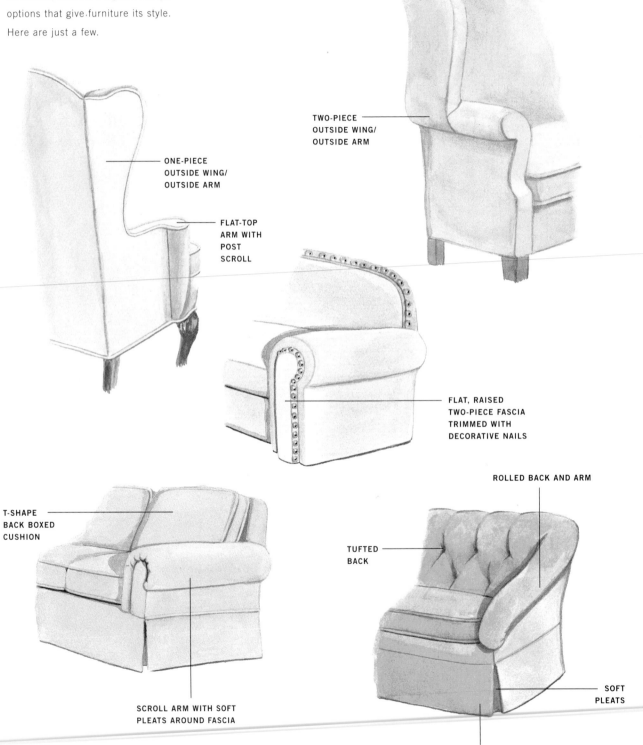

ONE-PIECE
OUTSIDE WING/
OUTSIDE ARM

FLAT-TOP
ARM WITH
POST
SCROLL

TWO-PIECE
OUTSIDE WING/
OUTSIDE ARM

FLAT, RAISED
TWO-PIECE FASCIA
TRIMMED WITH
DECORATIVE NAILS

T-SHAPE
BACK BOXED
CUSHION

ROLLED BACK AND ARM

TUFTED
BACK

SOFT
PLEATS

SCROLL ARM WITH SOFT
PLEATS AROUND FASCIA

CURVED FRONT CORNERS

tools and terms

If you sew you may recognize the names of some stitches, tools, materials, and terms used in this book. But don't be fooled! In many cases the same name will refer to a totally different item in the language of upholstery. Consider, for example, batting: Upholstery batting is coarse and stiff, designed to resist the pressures of the body. It's not soft or fluffy like the batting used in a quilt.

To assure that you're getting the correct items for the job, purchase upholstery tools, equipment, and materials from suppliers and stores that specialize in this craft.

Below is a glossary of upholstery terms you should know. They're listed alphabetically so you can find them quickly if you wish to refer to them as you work. Many terms explained only briefly here are explained in detail and illustrated in the chapters that relate to their use.

Allowance(s): An extra amount of fabric added to the visible dimensions of each section before cutting the new cover. Allowances provide a fitting tolerance and enable you to secure the cover; they're tacked to the frame or sewn together. A seam allowance is a specific type of allowance.

Basting: Temporary long, straight stitches made by hand or machine for the purpose of testing the fit of cover pieces or the alignment of a repeating pattern on the fabric.

Batting: The padding placed under the upholstery fabric.
✄Felted cotton comes in rolled sheets about $1/2$" thick. Except on the deck and lip, it should be covered with an interlining.
✄Polyester batting comes in rolled sheets $1/2$" and 1" thick; the thicker type should be separated into two $1/2$" layers. Polyester batting has a stabilizing surface finish and can be used without an interlining; it's the choice of most upholsterers.

Blind-tack: A method of tacking the fabric to the frame. The tacks are concealed by the fabric once it's turned or folded into its final position.

Burlap: A coarse jute fabric used as a base under stuffing and padding. Use 16-ounce burlap inside the frame over springs. Use 7- to 10-ounce burlap over the outside of the frame.

Chisel: A tool with a short blade that is beveled on both sides. Used to scrape dried-out foam stuffing from the frame.

Claw tool: A forked-end tool used to remove tacks and staples from the frame.

Cross-marking: The technique of making match-marks on adjoining old upholstery pieces before stripping. Cross-marks are later duplicated on the new upholstery pieces and used to align them on the frame and with one another when tacking or sewing.

Crowning: The technique of building up layers of loose stuffing, such as horsehair, in the center of tight seats and backs to ensure that the final shape will be full and firm. Each layer is larger than the one beneath; the top layer covers the entire area. Found on high-quality, or older, furniture.

Decking fabric: On a tight seat the decking fabric is the upholstery fabric. When the furniture has a loose seat cushion, you've the option of cutting the back section of the deck from heavy muslin or a cotton twill fabric.

Decorative nails: These can be used to secure the cover to the frame. When placed adjacent to one another, they can finish a raw edge. They can also be spaced apart along a turned edge or over a braid or gimp. Sometimes called *decorative tacks*, they come in many styles with plain or faceted heads.

Dust cover: A lightweight fabric, usually black cambric, tacked to the bottom of the furniture to conceal the webbing and prevent dust from penetrating up into the furniture. Cambric can be woven or nonwoven.

Edgestitch: Parallel rows of machine-made straight stitches that hold seam allowances open and eliminate the need for pressing. From the right side of the fabric, stitch on each side of the seamline $1/8$" from the seam.

Edgewire or spring edgewire: A wire frame attached to coiled springs in some furniture constructions. It defines the perimeter of the seat or back, providing a shape on which to build the upholstery.

Fox edging or edge roll: A thick cord covered with burlap, made in the same manner as welting. It's tacked around the frame to soften edges and keep the wood from abrading the upholstery fabric. Use a ³/₄"-diameter edging on backs and arms, and a 1¹/₂"-diameter edging on seats.

Hand stitches: A variety of stitches made by hand—such as the backstitch, blindstitch, and lock stitch—which are used for specific purposes during upholstery. Refer to Basic Construction Techniques, pages 54–76.

Interfacing: A stiff, woven, or nonwoven fabric used to add body to the skirts of upholstery.

Knots: A variety of knots such as clove-hitch, slip-knot, overhand knot, twin-tack, and cloverleaf are used to tie springs together and to the frame. Refer to Repairing the Innards, pages 47–50.

Liner: A layer of unbleached muslin or polyester batting placed over felted cotton batting.

Lining: Line skirts with sateen (cotton fabric).

Magnetic tack hammer: A special thin-headed hammer with a magnetic 10- to 14-ounce head used to slip-tack and tack materials to the frame. On some styles the nonmagnetic head has a soft, white plastic tip designed for tacking decorative nails.

Mallet: A rubber, rawhide, or wood hammer used to finalize the tacking process and secure tacking strips. Its softness protects the fabrics.

Needles: ✂Use curved needles with rounded points for hand-sewing woven fabrics. (Those with triangular points are for vinyl fabrics and leather—materials for the experienced upholsterer.) Use a 6"-long needle for heavy-duty sewing on the inner construction; use a 3"-long one for sewing the cover in places where a tacking strip or machine sewing isn't desired. ✂Use straight, single-pointed needles 12"–18" long, or use double-pointed buttoning needles to secure springs to webbing with spring twine. ✂Use an 8"–12" regulator needle to push extra batting into wrinkled upholstered corners as well as for tying springs and manipulating fabric into flexible tacking strips.

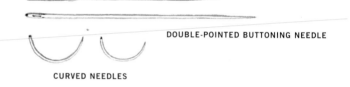

REGULATOR NEEDLE

DOUBLE-POINTED BUTTONING NEEDLE

CURVED NEEDLES

Padding: The layer of softening material just beneath the upholstery fabric. See **batting** on page 25 for the types to use.

TIPS FROM THE PROS

Many upholsterers use the words *stuffing* and *padding* interchangeably. For the purposes of this book's instructions, we've chosen to make a distinction. *Stuffing* refers to the cushioning materials layered over the springs. *Padding* refers to the softening materials installed directly under the upholstery fabric.

Pincers: Wide pliers used to strip off the old cover and to remove tacks and staples, as well as to grip and pull fabrics taut for tacking.

Pin-tack: A temporary method of attaching upholstery materials and fabrics to the frame using upholstery skewers or heavy pins in preparation for slip-tacking, tacking, or securing around flexible tacking strips.

Pleats: There are two kinds of pleats used in upholstery. ✂Shape fabric over and around curves (as on scroll arm fronts) by folding it into tapered pleats. ✂Use illusory pleats on upholstered skirts; these are not folded but consist of adjacent long, flat pieces placed over separate backdrops.

Repeat: The distance between two identical points of two identically oriented motifs on the fabric. Repeats can be horizontal and/or vertical.

Seam allowance: A designated allowance, usually $1/2$", that is added to the finished dimensions of pieces on an edge that will be sewn to another piece. Seam allowances are hidden on the wrong side of the cover pieces.

Shears: ✂Use large bent-handle shears 10"–12" long for cutting fabrics, stuffing, and batting. ✂Use tin snips to cut metal tacking strips.

Slashes: A variety of cuts used to make the fabric pieces fit together or fit around a part of the frame. ✂Use straight and notched slashes when sewing convex and concave seam allowances together. ✂Use Y-shaped slashes to make a cover fit around an attached exposed arm or back post.

Slip-tacking: A temporary method of attaching upholstery materials and fabrics to the frame. Drive the tacks or staples only partially into the frame; you'll drive them in all the way after making any necessary adjustments.

Springs: Two types of springs—coil and zigzag—provide a flexible support system for seats and backs.

Spring twine: Sometimes called *laidcord,* this waxed jute twine is $3/32$" thick. Use it to tie springs together.

Staple gun and staples: Use an electric staple gun to tack materials to the frame; it's faster and easier to use than a tack hammer and tacks. A hand-powered staple gun has too much kick to give accurate results; you won't be able to control it. Rent a heavy-duty gun if you wish.

Stuffing: Cushioning materials on top of springs. You can use horsehair, synthetic- or rubberized-hair, or solid foam in the body of the furniture. ✂For loose cushions use solid foam covered with a layer of polyester batting or use loose polyester wadding to fill the inner cushion. You can also ask a professional to make inside cushions from (1) polyester fibers mixed with down and feathers, (2) foam covered with polyester batting and then a mix of down and feathers, or (3) pocketed springs plus foam, polyester batting, and a mix of fibers, down, and feathers.

Tacking: A permanent method of attaching upholstery materials and fabrics to the frame.

Tacking strips: Available in three types, they allow you to do variations of blind-tacking while forming perfectly finished, concealed cut edges in the upholstery fabric. ✂Use $1/2$"-wide cardboard strips when blind-tacking pieces from the wrong side of the fabric, such as for the top edge of an outside arm. ✂Use rigid metal strips with protruding spikes to finish any straight outside edge of the upholstery; work with the right side of the fabric facing you. ✂Use flexible metal strips, which have notched edges that can bend around curves and a jaw that clamps the fabric into place, to finish straight or curved outside edges. Work with the right side of the fabric facing you.

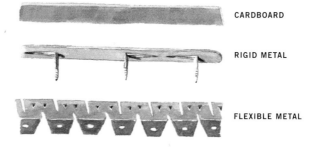

CARDBOARD

RIGID METAL

FLEXIBLE METAL

Tacks: Use tacks to attach materials to the frame. Upholstery tacks are sterilized, because the professional upholsterer spits a tack onto the magnetized tack hammer from a small quantity held in the mouth. In general use #9 tacks for a hardwood frame, #12 tacks for a softwood frame, and #2 or #3 tacks for delicate applications such as tacking fabric around a fascia. Keep a variety of sizes on hand.

tools and terms

Trims: A wide variety of narrow, decorative fabrics—such as braids, gimp, fringes, tassels, and cordings—used to enhance the upholstery. Some trims can be used to cover the tacks on fabric edges next to an exposed, finished frame.

Upholstery fabric: The decorative top fabric covering the furniture. Sometimes there's a plain fabric fused to the wrong side of an upholstery fabric in order to give strength and stability to a fabric that is otherwise inappropriate for a cover.

Upholstery horses and worktable: Use horses to raise the furniture to a comfortable height while you're working. When the furniture can be upright, rest the legs on the upholstered arms attached to the top of the horses. When the furniture needs to be turned on its side, add a worktable—a detachable top of upholstered plywood—to span the distance between the horses to make a solid work surface.

Upholstery skewers: Use skewers—$3^{1}/_{2}$"-long pins with an open-ring head—to pin-tack materials to the partially upholstered furniture. You can easily substitute heavy glass-head pins or even hat pins.

Webbing: A coarse, tightly woven $3^{1}/_{2}$"-wide band of jute fabric used to weave a supporting base for springs and all other materials used in upholstery. In post-1960 furniture you may find rubberized webbing strips, which replace springs and serve as support for the various other materials.

Webbing stretcher: Use this tool to pull and stretch new webbing tightly over the frame. It's available with a common, straight handle or with a bent handle.

Welting: Welting—sometimes called *piping*—consists of a bias strip of upholstery fabric stitched tightly around a firm cord about $^{3}/_{16}$" in diameter. The long edges of the bias extend beyond the stitching to form a $^{1}/_{2}$" seam allowance, which can be sewn into seams or tacked to furniture edges.

Zippers: Use heavy-duty zippers to close cushion covers. Traditional metal upholstery zippers have black or beige tape and gold teeth. Polyester-coil zippers come in many colors. Some suppliers will custom-cut a zipper to your needs.

essential tools and equipment

To get off to a good start, assemble the equipment listed below; you can add more as the need arises. Starred* items are explained in the glossary; others are common household items.

- Chalk (tailor's wax or chalk, or blackboard chalk)
- Claw tool or staple lifter*
- Curved upholstery needles, 3" and 6" long*
- Hot-glue gun and glue, or clear spray foam adhesive (makes a fine line of glue)
- Mallet*
- Magnetic tack hammer*
- Pins
- Retractable blade knife
- Screwdrivers (Phillips and slotted)
- Seam ripper
- Sewing machine (home or industrial)
- Staple gun (electric) and staples*
- Straight upholstery needles, 6" and 12" long*
- Tape measures (retractable metal and vinyl types)
- Thimble
- Thread (heavy duty for hand sewing; machine upholstery thread)
- Webbing stretcher*
- Upholstery tacks, #4 and #12*
- Yardstick or straightedge

making upholsterer's horses and a worktable

If you're upholstering small items, you may only need horses. Adding a worktable on top of the horses, however, makes it easier to handle larger pieces. To protect your furniture and keep it from sliding around, upholster these supports with heavy canvas or carpet.

YOU NEED

For Horses and Worktable
  Pencil and straightedge
  #12 tacks and a tack hammer;
  or a staple gun and staples
For Horses
  2 pieces heavy canvas or carpet,
  cut 56" x 18"
  2 pieces 1 x 12 pine board,
  cut 4' 4" long
  Retractable blade knife
  2 purchased sawhorses that are
  4' long by a comfortable work height
  16 inside corner braces, 2" size with
  ¹/₂" wood screws
For Worktable
  1 piece heavy canvas or carpet,
  cut 6" larger than plywood in length
  and width
  1 piece plywood, cut 4' x 5' or
  4' x 8'

Make two horses and one worktable as follows: Place the heavy canvas or carpet on a table or clean floor, wrong side up. Place the board, centered, on top. If using carpet, draw a straight line out to each edge of the carpet at each corner of the board.

Following the lines, cut out a square from each corner using the knife. If using canvas, keep the piece whole. △

Turn the board and cover over and slip-tack the top of the cover to the board. Turn the board and cover wood side up.

Fold the cover over one edge of the board and tack, working from the center to each corner; repeat on the opposite edge. If using canvas, fold the fabric at the ends as shown. ▽

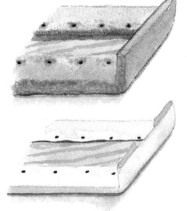

Fold each end of the cover onto the board and tack. ▽

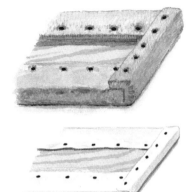

Turn the board over and remove the slip-tacking.

To finish the horses, turn the boards over again. Center the top of a sawhorse on the back of each board. Position 4 corner braces along each side, and then screw the board and sawhorse together. ▽

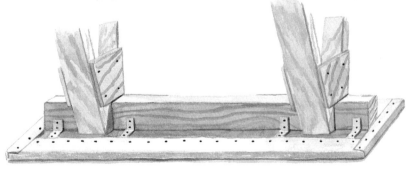

the parts of the cover

Before you get to work, you need a plan. Take a good look at the piece of furniture you want to reupholster. While the piece is still intact, you can see how the cover is constructed, begin to understand the complexity of the task ahead, and think about the kind of fabric you want to use. Begin by identifying and listing the parts of the cover.

Make some simple line drawings of your furniture, as described below. They don't have to be works of art; they're just for your own reference. Later you'll use them again when you measure the parts of the cover to determine how large to cut each piece and how much fabric to buy.

MAKING SIMPLE DRAWINGS OF FURNITURE

Remove any loose cushions from the furniture and set them aside. Draw the outline of the furniture, then add the primary outline of each section of the cover. Draw details such as internal seamlines, mitered front corners, and welting, if any. (Welting can be drawn as two parallel lines, as shown, or as one heavier pencil line.) Draw the furniture from as many angles as needed to record all the pieces; two three-quarter views (one front and one back) are usually sufficient.

Inside each outlined shape write the name of the cover piece. Label any construction details such as seamlines and mitered corners. Note the placement of any welting or decorative trims and nails. If you're reupholstering a wide piece of furniture, read Measuring and Estimating, pages 36–37, and incorporate the piecing seamlines into your drawing. (Their placement can be approximate; you'll just need to account for them.)

Your furniture might have components not featured on this wing chair, such as a skirt with illusory pleats, softly draped pleats on the arm, or a solid seat. If not, you might decide to incorporate them into the new cover anyway. Be sure to draw and label each area and detail. There's no need to include the fine details of the exposed wood.

Draw any loose cushions separately, indicating the position of the double box area that contains the zipper.

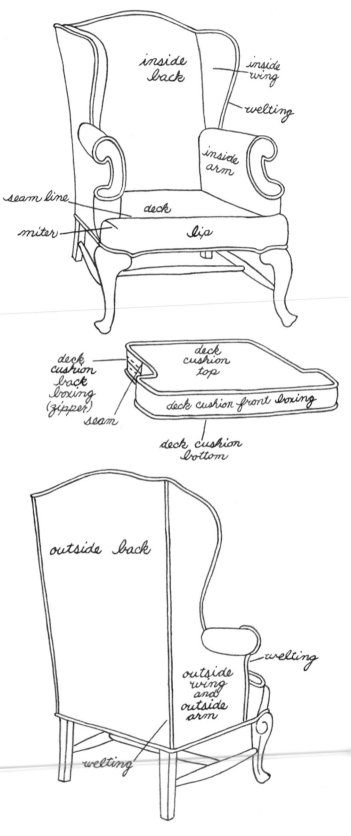

✄Take photographs of your furniture from different angles before you start the reupholstery process. They'll be an invaluable reference while you work.

✄If you photograph the appropriate angles, you can place tracing paper over the photos and draw your furniture.

✄A magazine photo of a piece of furniture similar to your own can be used instead of a photo that you take. Adjust the details to match those of your furniture.

✄If you want a larger drawing, take your tracings to a copy center and have them enlarged to a size that will allow you to draw welting, seams, and other fine details that need to be recorded.

✄If you're upholstering a wide piece of furniture, name and list each portion of any sections that will be pieced (inside back center panel, inside back side panel, etc.).

At this time you should also measure all the edges of the furniture to which welting will be applied. Write the total length (in yards) of welting needed on the chart.

You'll refer often to this chart as you reupholster. It will be especially helpful when you're ready to make a cutting layout and calculate the fabric yardage.

LISTING THE COVER PIECES

Using the chart at right as an example, make a chart with three wide columns to help you organize your pieces. In the first column write the name of each piece labeled in your drawings and the number needed of each. In the second and third columns, make space for four measurements as shown. In the second measurement space of these columns, write the length and width, respectively. Later you'll add the seam and tacking allowances to these columns and total each entry to find the cutting dimensions. ▷

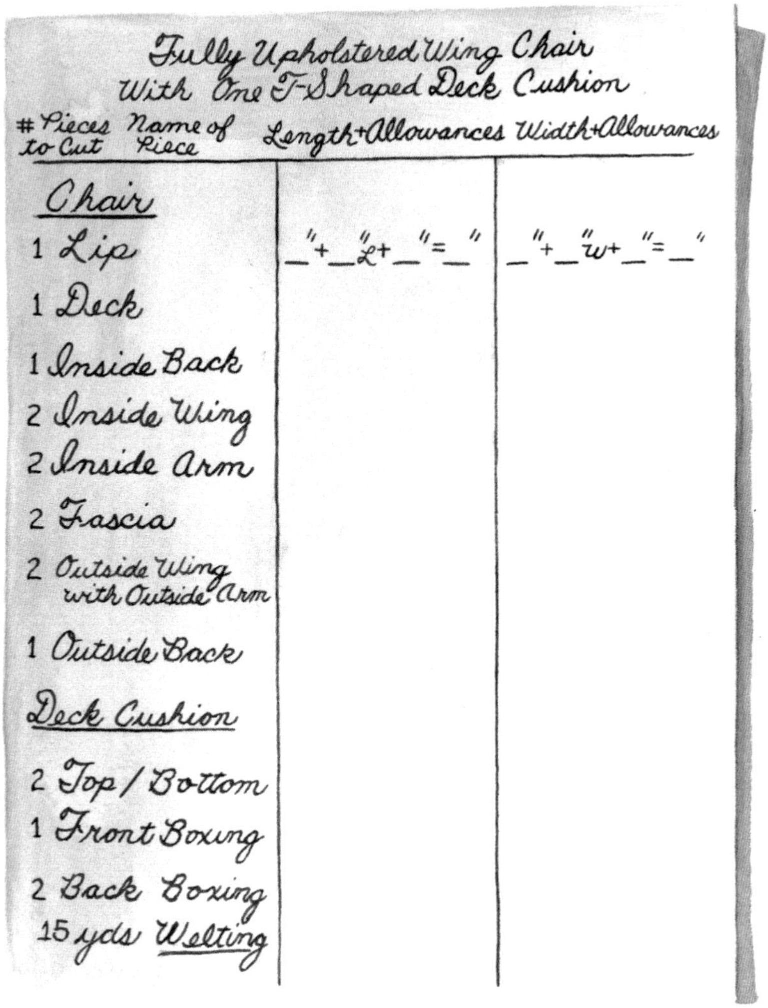

Fully Upholstered Wing Chair
With One T-Shaped Deck Cushion

# Pieces to Cut / Name of Piece	Length+Allowances	Width+Allowances
Chair		
1 Lip	_"+_ℓ+_"=_"	_"+_w+_"=_"
1 Deck		
1 Inside Back		
2 Inside Wing		
2 Inside Arm		
2 Fascia		
2 Outside Wing with Outside Arm		
1 Outside Back		
Deck Cushion		
2 Top / Bottom		
1 Front Boxing		
2 Back Boxing		
15 yds Welting		

the fabric treatment

Choosing the right fabric means much more than just finding a fabric you love. The color, style, and type of fabric you select, along with how you position it on the various parts of the furniture, all have as much to do with the ultimate success of your project as does your skill in doing the work.

SELECTING FABRIC

Although a solid color with no pattern to match may seem the easiest choice for beginners, it really isn't. Plain fabrics aren't forgiving: They tend to showcase errors, so unless you've some proficiency in draping fabric, choose an upholstery fabric with a small motif or pattern. Excellent first choices include such fabrics as a bicolor twill, a small multicolor print, or a small-pattern Jacquard (a fabric with a woven-in motif, such as damask). Look for a medium-weight fabric in medium-to-dark colors with a matte surface; pale colors and shiny surfaces tend to reveal any dimples or bumps in the upholstery.

TIPS FROM THE PROS

✂ Be sure the scale of the motif, plaid, or stripes is appropriate for the size of the furniture: Will it overwhelm it or look lost?
✂ Choose a fabric in keeping with the style of the furniture and its intended use.
✂ Be sure that four or more thicknesses of the fabric will fit under the presser foot of your sewing machine.

ORIENTING THE FABRIC ON YOUR FURNITURE

If you have experience sewing, you may think that you have the choice whether to place a fabric on the furniture with the lengthwise grain running perpendicular or parallel to the floor. Not so in upholstery, where the fabrics are designed to run in a particular direction.

Vertically Run Fabric

Most fabrics are intended to be placed on the furniture with the lengthwise grain (selvages) perpendicular to the floor; this orientation is called *vertically run*. When vertically run fabrics cover a wide area, they must be seamed together. Vertically run fabrics may have one-way patterns, stripes, plaids, or random or allover patterns. The motifs on these fabrics are woven or printed so they'll appear pleasing (and right side up) when properly oriented. Depending on the particular pattern, you may or may not be able to select which direction is up. ▽

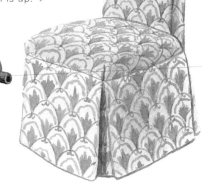

Railroaded Fabric

Some fabrics are designed to be turned crosswise (railroaded) on the furniture with the lengthwise grain (selvages) running parallel to the floor. On railroaded fabrics a directional pattern is printed or woven on the crosswise grain, and when the fabric is placed on the furniture, the pattern runs perpendicular to the floor. With railroaded fabrics you can cover a wide area seamlessly, so they're good choices for sofas. Railroaded fabrics often feature stripes, or plaids that have a dominant stripe on the crosswise grain; these stripes will be vertical when placed on the furniture. ▽

✄Don't place a striped fabric going around the furniture—no professional would ever do so.

✄Check the selvages of any printed fabric. Arrows printed there at regular intervals are a handy aid in cutting out pieces using a consistent vertical orientation. Although it's obvious the stripe in this illustration is to be vertically run because it's parallel to the selvage; the arrow lets you know which way is up.▽

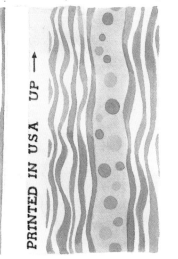

ALIGNING AND MATCHING FABRIC PIECES

Many novice upholsterers are shy about matching fabric patterns, but it need not be either challenging or daunting. Depending upon the scale and nature of the fabric pattern, and the size of the pieces you're working with, you may not need to be concerned about aligning or matching the motif on one section to those on adjacent sections. (Refer to photos 49–50, page 126.)

✄On smaller motifs, 12" or less, align the inside pieces vertically with each other, and then align the outside pieces to the inside ones.

✄On large motifs, 12" or more, it's more important to center the motif within each piece, independent of adjoining pieces. This gives the most pleasing effect.

✄On plaids always align the vertical lines from front to back at the centers, and align the horizontal lines all around the circumference of the furniture. Match the plaid of a skirt to the upholstered front and, as much as possible, to the side and back pieces above it.

✄On stripes match all the vertical lines from piece to piece.

✄If you're seaming widths of fabric to cover a wide back or

seat, be sure to match any pattern or align any motifs horizontally, maintaining their repeat—the results should appear seamless. Upholstery fabric is designed so that the horizontal repeat will continue evenly when widths are joined at the selvage. To see how far inside the edge to place the seamline, lap the right edge of one width over the left edge of another, and fold it under as necessary to continue the pattern; measure the amount folded under.

✄If your furniture has loose seat cushions and your fabric repeat is 12" or more, you must plan ahead because you upholster the lip and inside back before you make the cushions. First decide how the fabric will be placed on the top of the cushion. Then plan to match the front edge of the cushion top to the top edge of the cushion boxing. Then match the top edge of the drop of the lip to the bottom of the boxing. Once this portion of the repeat is determined, you can cut out the lip and continue cutting out the cover pieces as you need them.

CUSTOMIZING WING PIECES TO SUIT THE FABRIC

When using a fabric with a large motif for a wing chair with a one-piece outside wing/outside arm, consider cutting the outside wing separately from the outside arm so that you can center a motif on each section.

✄To turn a one-piece outside wing/outside arm into two pieces, cut horizontally across the stripped cover piece, extending the line of the top edge of the outside arm to the back edge. Refer to these pieces when estimating fabric (see pages 36–42),

✄When you cut out the two new outside pieces, center the large motif in each section, adding a 4" allowance to the bottom edge of the outside wing piece and to the top edge of the outside arm piece for later adjustment. ▽

USING TRIMS

When considering trim for upholstery, ask yourself two questions: (1) How will the trim be applied—inserted between pieces of the cover, applied on top, or both? (2) Which types of lines will it follow—curved, straight, or both?

Different trims have different properties: Some have a lip or flange that must be concealed between layers of fabric. Some must be glued or hand-sewn on top or attached with decorative nails. Some trims are flexible and will follow a curve; others are suitable only for straight edges. Most upholstery trims are applied to the furniture when the cover is in place, not to the cover pieces before they're installed. However, if you're using trim to border a skirt hem or cushion top or boxing, you can probably sew it on by machine before attaching the skirt or sewing the cushion together.

Welting

Welting—cord attached to a flat flange (also called a *lip)*—can twist and turn as needed. You can make welting by covering cord with bias strips of the cover fabric or a contrasting fabric. You can also purchase welting; both fabric-covered and decorative cord styles are available. Strictly speaking, because welting is applied as the cover is installed and it defines so many structural lines, it isn't considered a trim by upholsters. Nonetheless, it provides a visual finish that enhances the upholstery. Welting is typically inserted along the outer edges of upholstered pieces, between some interior sections, and around the perimeter of loose cushions; the flange must be concealed. Welting protects the edges of the upholstery from wear. Refer to page 73 for directions for making welting.

TIPS FROM THE PROS

✂ For a less expected finish, combine two different sizes of welting; the smaller one should be one-third or one-quarter the size of the larger one. Layer the flanges, placing the smaller cord just inside the larger one, and tack or sew to the upholstery as one piece.

✂ When combining two weltings, consider using contrasting fabrics, or use one fabric and one decorative cord, or try two different decorative cords.

Decorative Cording

Decorative cordings come in many diameters and textures, in solid or multicolor twists. Some have a lip and can be used as welting. If cording has no lip, it must be applied on top of the finished upholstery, either with glue or hand stitches; it can also be draped, swagged, and tied—options you might use to trim coordinating accessories even though they might be inappropriate for the upholstery itself.

Many cording designs are available both with and without a lip, which is handy if you wish to apply a trim both ways. Both styles will conform to any curve. Often coordinating fringes, medallions, and tassels are available to use in conjunction with cording. ▽

Braid

A braid, contrary to what you might expect, is a narrow, woven band of fabric—similar to ribbon. Braids vary in width from $1/2$" to several inches. They won't follow curves and should be used only to trim straight edges; however, they can be mitered at corners, so they're a good choice for bordering cushion tops. As with gimp, braid can be sewn, glued, or tacked in place, and it's often used to conceal the unfinished edge of the cover on furniture with an exposed frame. ▽

Gimp

Gimp is composed of a group of narrow cords looped and stitched together in a decorative pattern. There are many styles available, in both single colors and multicolors, in a variety of widths. Gimp has a right and wrong side: The right side has the raised pattern, the wrong side is flat, and chain stitches hold the cord design in place. Gimp can be sewn, glued, or tacked in place. it's often used to conceal the unfinished edges of the cover fabric on furniture with an exposed frame; a $3/8$" or $1/2$" width is perfect for this, and wider gimp is good for trimming skirts, cushions, and boxing borders. Gimp follows curves well, although different styles and widths have varying flexibility. Coordinating fringe is often available to use in conjunction with gimp. △

measuring and estimating

Get out your tape measure, calculator, and pencil, and don't be daunted by the prospect of doing some math. Although you may be tempted to forge ahead to a more gratifying part of the reupholstery process, the time you spend taking accurate measurements is time well spent. With good measurements you can calculate the amount of fabric you'll need, thus avoiding costly or frustrating inaccurate purchases. You'll also have a record of the original upholstery to compare your work to, which can be helpful should you find that you need to replace or supplement the inner materials.

MEASURING

Measure your furniture before purchasing the new fabric and before stripping off the old cover. Do this even if you purchase fabrics following a standard yardage chart. You'll need the measurements of the individual parts of the cover when you cut the new fabric.

Taking the Measurements

Measure each section of the cover at its widest and longest points. Measure the visible dimensions (the area that you can see); don't reach inside the crevices with your tape measure (refer to photo 2, page 114). Use your line drawings (refer to page 30) to record the dimensions as you measure; add arrows and a circle to each section as shown to keep the measurements clear.

If you're upholstering a sofa with vertically run fabric (refer to page 32), you'll have to piece the fabric in order to span the width of the seat, back, and skirt. Take the time to plan where the seams will fall. Avoid placing a vertical seam up the center of a sofa. Instead, use three panels of fabric, placing one in the center and one at each end.
✂If the sofa has a solid seat or a single loose cushion, make the center panel the full width of the fabric, and the outer panels equal to one another in width.
✂If the sofa has multiple loose cushions, make the seamlines on the panels of the deck, backs, and wide skirt pieces align with the junctions of the cushions.
✂In all cases the center panel should be the same width on the inside back, outside back, deck or seat, front, and skirt; the side panels will vary to reflect the configuration of the arms.

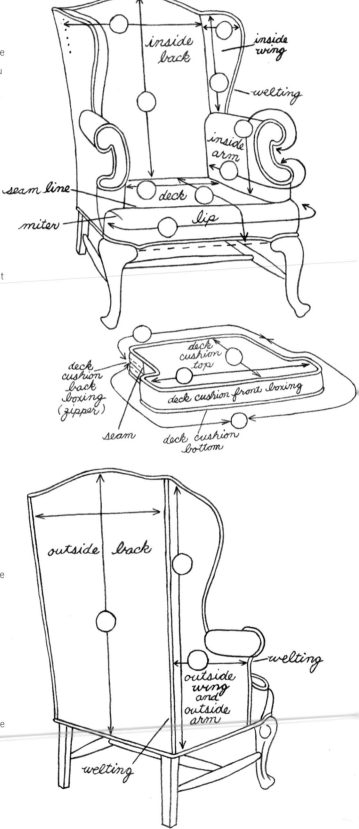

Transfer the measurements to your chart, placing each in the appropriate column. You'll add the allowances in the next step.

TIPS FROM THE PROS

✄If you know that the stuffing and padding inside your furniture needs extensive rebuilding, measure for the cover pieces after the inner reconstruction is complete.

Identifying Allowances

An *allowance* is the extra amount of fabric added to the visible dimensions of each section before cutting the new cover. Allowances provide a fitting tolerance, enabling you to refine the alignment of any fabric pattern and secure the cover; they're tacked to the frame or sewn together. The standard seam allowance is $1/2$". A number of wider tacking allowances, which permit you to shape and fit the cover as you install it, are described below.

Adding Allowances to the Measurements

Use the following general rules to add the appropriate seam or tacking allowance to the different edges of the cover pieces. A few examples from the wing chair shown are given for each type of allowance; in most cases these allowances will be the same for similar pieces on different styles of furniture. Cover pieces that you might encounter on other types of furniture are preceded by "Also:". If your furniture has a pleated skirt, refer to page 53 to plan the allowances.

To better understand the reasons for the different allowances, read the chapter Putting on the Cover, pages 77–111; it will help you analyze which allowances to use for your furniture. If in doubt, add a larger allowance—the worst that will happen is that you'll buy more fabric than you need; you trim the excess allowances as you work anyway. More is always safe!

Add the allowances to your chart.

Add a $1/2$" allowance to all edges that can be sewn using a standard seam allowance: *Fascia,* from bottom of top scroll to top of bottom scroll. *Inside arm,* edge adjacent to the fascia. *Cushion covers,* all edges except the ends of the boxing.

Also: *For a U-shape seam on a T-deck, or a non-T deck,* add a $1/2$" allowance to the front edge of the deck and the back edge of the lip. *For a gathered skirt,* add a $1/2$" allowance to the top and ends of each panel.

Add a 1" allowance to any edge, or part of an edge, requiring an extra-wide allowance for special handling: *Fascia,* area on the outside edge between the scrolls.

Also: *For a gathered skirt,* add a 1" allowance to the bottom of each panel for the hem.

Add a 2" allowance to any edge that gets trimmed close to the tacking on an exposed frame, wrapped around a tacking strip, or tacked around a post or rail without first disappearing into the crevices along the seat or inside back: *Outside back,* all edges. *Inside back,* top edge. *Inside wing,* top and front edges. *Inside arm,* top and vertical scroll post edges.
✄*For a T-shape deck,* add 2" allowance to the front of the deck and the back of the lip so you can fit them around the inside arm.

Also: *For a front border,* add 2" allowance to all edges. *For an applied fascia,* add 2" allowance to all edges.

Add a 4" allowance to any edge that disappears into the crevices along the seat or inside back, or anytime you're in doubt as to how much allowance to add: *Inside back,* sides and bottom edges. *Inside wing,* inside and bottom edges. *Inside arm,* inside and bottom edges.

TIPS FROM THE PROS

✄You might find it easier to keep track of which edge gets which allowance if you make a sketch of each piece and then add the appropriate allowance onto each edge. You don't have to draw the refined shape of each piece; just sketch a rectangle in the approximate proportion of your recorded visible measurements. Note the allowance depth on each edge, and then transfer it to your chart.
✄Remember to add seam allowances to the seamed edges of any panels that will be pieced to span your furniture.

measuring and estimating

Finalizing the Dimensions

Using the chart below as an example, add the allowances to your chart if you've not already done so. For each piece, total the allowances-plus-length, and enter the figure on your chart. Total the dimensions to which you'll cut each piece of your cover. ▽

# Pieces to Cut	Name of Piece	Length+Allowances	Width+Allowances
	Fully Upholstered Wing Chair with One T-Shaped Deck Cushion		
	Chair		
1	*Lip*	½" + 11½" + 2" = 13½"	2" + 35"w + 2" = 39"
1	*Deck*	4" + 15" + ½" = 19½"	4" + 22" + 4" = 30"
1	*Inside Back*	2" + 33" + 4" = 39"	4" + 21 + 4" = 29"
2	*Inside Wing*		
2	*Inside Arm*		
2	*Fascia*		
2	*Outside Wing with Outside Arm*		
1	*Outside Back*		

IDENTIFYING THE PARTS OF THE FABRIC

When you upholster, you stretch and mold the cover fabric tightly over the furniture. To assure that the cover conforms to the furniture and any motifs align properly, each piece must be cut squarely from the yardage—with the lengthwise edges parallel to the selvages (or, if the piece isn't rectangular, with the vertical center parallel to the selvages). Familiarize yourself with the names and definitions of the fabric parts now; you'll use this information as you calculate the yardage.

Selvages are the parallel, woven edges that run the length of the fabric. Often the selvage is tight or the area immediately adjacent to it isn't printed. If so, the unusable portions should be subtracted from the **usable width** of the fabric.

The **lengthwise grain** lies parallel to the selvages. It's the most stable grain. Find the straight grain by measuring two points equidistant from one selvage.

The **crosswise grain** lies perpendicular to the selvages. It isn't as strong as the lengthwise grain. Find the crosswise grain by aligning one side of an L- or T-square with the selvage.

The **bias** lies at a 45-degree angle to the selvages. It isn't stable but stretches and molds easily. Use fabric strips cut on the bias to cover welting; they'll provide the smoothest and most flexible covering. Use a 45-degree right-angle triangle to find the bias (place one leg along the selvage, and the hypotenuse will lie on the bias).

A **repeat** is the interval at which a motif or decorative pattern is duplicated on the fabric. Most patterns have both a horizontal and vertical repeat; stripes have one or the other. Repeats are measured in inches.

The **length of a repeat** is the distance, measured on the lengthwise grain, between two identical parts of a motif. Fabric manufacturers list this dimension as the **vertical repeat** in their product specifications.

The **width of a repeat** is the distance, measured on the crosswise grain, between two identical parts of a motif. Fabric manufacturers list this dimension as the **horizontal repeat** in their product specifications.

TIPS FROM THE PROS

✂ To determine a fabric's vertical repeat, find a prominent feature of the motif (the tip of a leaf, for instance) and mark it with a pin on two consecutive vertical motifs. Measure the distance between the pins. Determine the horizontal repeat in the same manner. ▽

CALCULATING FABRIC YARDAGE

Once you've determined the measurements of all your cover pieces and found the size of any repeats on your fabric, you're ready to calculate the amount of fabric you'll need. You can use a chart to estimate the yardage, or you can make more exact calculations mathematically.

Estimating Yardage from a Chart

Having an approximate idea of the amount of fabric needed will help you plan the cost of your upholstery. You can use the chart on the next page to quickly make an estimate after you decide which type of furniture below your piece most closely resembles.

measuring and estimating

		No Skirt	Standard Kick Pleat
A	Round Ottoman (up to 33" diameter)	$1^1/4$	$2^1/2$
B	Standard Ottoman (to 23" x 23")	$1^3/4$	$2^3/4$
C	Large Ottoman (to 27" x 27")	$3/4$	$3^3/4$
D	Dining Room Chair with Drop Seat	$2^1/4$	
E	Armless Boudoir Chair	6	$7^1/2$
F	French Provincial Armchair	$2^1/2$	
G	Barrelback Chair	8	9
H	Fully Upholstered Armchair with Tight Back	8	9
I	Armchair with Removable Back Cushion	11	12
J	Wing Chair with Removable Deck Cushion	11	12
K	Chaise Lounge with Tight Seat and One Arm	15	17
L	Chaise Lounge with Removable Deck Cushion	14	$15^1/2$
M	2-Cushion Love Seat with Tight Back (to 72" wide)	14	16
N	2-Cushion Sofa with Tight Back (to 91" wide)	17	19
O	1-Cushion Camelback Sofa (to 86" wide)	14	16
P	3-Cushion Sofa (to 86" wide)	17	19
Q	2-Cushion Sofa with 2 Removable Back Cushions (to 86" wide)	21	24
R	3-Cushion Sofa with 3 Removable Back Cushions (to 86" wide)	21	24

The yardages listed above are for 54"-wide plain fabric placed vertically on the furniture (with the selvages perpendicular to the floor).

✂ For shirred and box-pleated skirt options, add the following additional yardage to standard kick-pleat skirt yardage:

    ottoman/chair—1 yard

    chaise/love seat—3 yards

    sofa—4 yards

✂ For contrasting welting, add the following additional yardage:

    ottoman—1 yard

    chair—$1^1/2$ yards

    chaise—2 yards

    love seat—$2^1/2$ yards

    sofa—3 yards

Note: One yard of 54"-wide fabric yields 12 yards of welting cut in $1^3/4$"-wide strips.

✂ The following yardage may be deducted when using a different deck fabric:

    chair—1 yard

    chaise—2 yards

    love seat—2 yards

    sofa—3 yards

Considering the Fabric Repeat

Fabrics with a repeating pattern of more than 3" usually require additional fabric. To determine a fabric's vertical and horizontal repeat, follow the directions on page 38. Once you've estimated the yardage you'd need if using plain fabric, you can use the chart below to estimate the requirements for a fabric with a repeating pattern. To use this chart, first add the fabric's vertical and horizontal repeats together (for example, a 10" vertical repeat plus its 17" horizontal repeat gives a 27" total). Then find the appropriate entry on the chart, and increase the plain fabric estimate by the percentage indicated.

Fabric Width	Plain Fabric	3"–14" Repeat	15"–19" Repeat	20"–27" Repeat	28"–36" Repeat	37"–45" Repeat	46"–54" Repeat
54"	0%	10%	15%	20%	25%	30%	35%
50"–52"	10%	20%	25%	30%	35%	40%	45%

Drawing a Yardage-Estimating Diagram

It's easier to calculate the total yardage needed to cover a piece of furniture if you draw an estimating diagram, which will help you visualize the amount of fabric needed to accommodate all the pieces and allow for the proper repeats. This diagram is similar to a cutting layout found in a commercial pattern, but for upholstery the pieces should be arranged on the layout in the order in which you'll cut them. If your fabric has a large repeat, the cutting layout may not be the most economical use of the fabric, but it will be the most practical.

Use graph paper with 6–10 squares to the inch for your diagram. Decide upon a working scale (for instance, decide that each square on the graph paper represents 2" of fabric; 18 squares equal 1 yard). Tape sheets together to make a length that will represent the yardage you've estimated using the charts; you can add more as needed.

The first part of the diagram: First, using the scale you've chosen, draw two parallel lines to indicate the usable width of your fabric—the width minus selvages and any unprinted area along them. Label these lines *selvages*. Next, at one end draw a line perpendicular to the first two, to represent one end of the yardage.

If your fabric has a repeating pattern or motif, determine width and length of repeats (refer to page 38). Decide which part of the motif you wish to feature, or center, on each piece of your cover. Mark it on the motif lying closest to the left edge, and measure its distance from this edge (don't measure across any portion of the fabric near the selvage that isn't usable).

Near the end on your scale drawing, draw a small triangle the appropriate distance from the left edge to represent the center of the motif. Point a corner of the triangle away from the end to indicate which end is up on the fabric. Draw additional triangles to indicate the centers of the repeats on the remainder of your scale drawing.

Record the length and width of the repeat on the grid. (If your fabric has no motif, you should still indicate which way is up at intervals along your diagram by marking triangles or small arrows; the intervals need not be regular.) ▽

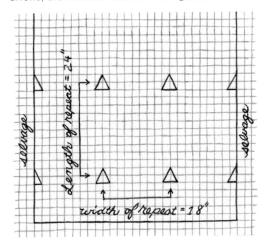

The second part of the diagram: Next, draw the individual cover pieces to scale on a separate piece of graph paper. Refer to your measurement chart, and draw duplicate pieces when more than one is needed. Label each piece with the appropriate name and measurements. If you're planning to center a motif, draw an orientation triangle on each piece, centering it within the visible portion as defined by the seam and tacking allowances. Otherwise, just indicate the desired up orientation. Cut out all the pieces, including the outline. ▽

measuring and estimating

As explained on page 33, it's essential to plan the position of a large repeat on the lip of the deck and any seat cushions simultaneously. To then plan the position of the repeat on the inside back, mark a cushion line on the inside back paper piece; place this line the depth of the cushion boxing above the bottom tacking allowance, and match the repeat above it. Refer to pages 32–33 for more about orienting pieces.

TIPS FROM THE PROS

✂ If you draw interior lines on the cover pieces to indicate the amount of allowance given on each edge, you'll find it easier to center motifs.

✂ If you're working with a striped or plaid fabric, draw lines at intervals on the fabric graph to represent the repeat of the dominant stripe. If your fabric is railroaded, draw the lines across the graph. Center a line lengthwise on each cover piece.

✂ If your fabric has motifs to match, use transparent graph paper for the cut-out pieces, or mark the motif center on the fabric graph with a dark pen that reads through them.

Assemble the diagram: Arrange the cut-out pieces on the fabric graph, aligning the repeat center triangles on the cutouts with those on the fabric graph and placing all the "up" indicators in the same orientation. If you're working with a railroaded fabric arrange the cut-out pieces with their up indicators pointed toward the same selvage.

Make the arrangement as efficient as possible. Keep the edges of the cut-outs parallel to the lines on the fabric graph (the graph lines need not align). You can plan to cut smaller pieces from the areas not used next to larger ones.

When the arrangement is complete, tape the paper layers together. ▷

TIPS FROM THE PROS

✂ There's no need to draw pieces for the bias strips for welting; you can use the chart on page 40 to calculate the yardage you'll need, and add this amount to the calculation you'll make next.

✂ Don't give in to the temptation to cut the bias strips from the excess fabric around the cover pieces. The amount of fabric you'll save isn't worth the time spent piecing the strips together, and the more piecing you do, the more bulky seams you'll have interrupting the welting.

Calculating the Yardage

Along one edge of your fabric graph, count the number of squares used in the arrangement. Multiply this by the assigned number of inches-per-square to calculate the total number of inches needed; divide this number by 36 to find the required yardage. For instance, if your diagram covers a length of 180 squares on the fabric graph and the scale is 2-inches-per-square, multiply 180 by 2 to see that you'll need 360 inches of fabric, or 10 yards. Add the amount needed for welting to the total. Because you prepared a customized plan, there's no need to add any further overage amounts for matching or centering a motif.

TIPS FROM THE PROS

✂ Buy some extra fabric anyway—you'll feel more confident. And if you should make a cutting error, you won't have to reorder.

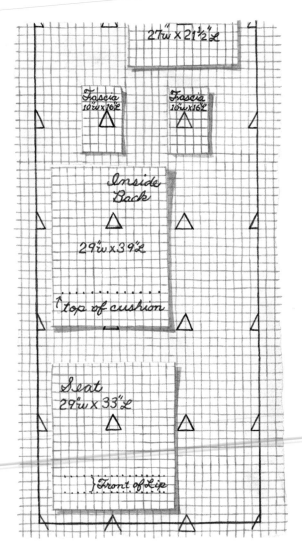

stripping the old fabric

Although everything you do to prepare for reupholstery is important, stripping the old cover from your furniture is probably the most important step. there's no mystery to the process itself—think of it as undressing the furniture, removing first the last piece put on (refer to photos 4–5, page 115). If you work methodically and document the process, you'll be all set to reverse it and recover the chair with confidence.

If you've questions about the nature or purpose of the materials you encounter, look through other parts of this book for more information. Read the chapters Repairing the Innards and Putting on the Cover to learn about reusing or replacing materials, especially if you're redoing an older piece.

ABOUT THE STRIPPING PROCESS

As you remove the cover and its underlying layers, you'll see how the upholstery was put together and really begin to understand how to replicate it. Whatever the style of your furniture, you always strip from the outermost layer inward, removing the pieces in reverse order from that in which they were attached— if you find yourself trying to pull a piece from under another one, you're jumping the gun. The order in which to strip is given later in this chapter; once you begin, you'll find it pretty obvious.

Work with care so that you can identify, label, and save all the pieces you remove. Some, such as padding, stuffing, and inner cushions, might be reusable; others, such as the cover itself, become cutting guides. All will be invaluable references as you recover your furniture. As you strip, take photographs or sketch details that might be forgotten by the time you're ready to duplicate them. Make notes, especially about which kinds of tacking strip are used.

When stripping the inside back, inside wings, inside arms, and deck, you should always remove foam stuffing. However, remove any real or synthetic hair stuffing, and the padding and muslin over it, only if necessary to repair the frame or springs. You can reinforce the burlap that supports them from the outside and supplement them with a new layer of padding.

TIPS FROM THE PROS

✄ If you're stripping an older chair, the cover might be hand-sewn along the outer edges. You can probably use rigid or flexible metal tacking strips to secure these portions of your new cover.

GETTING STARTED

Stripping is a dusty process, so work in an appropriate place. Consider wearing a dust mask and goggles. Set up your upholsterer's horses. Have a table nearby on which to fold, label, and store the old cover pieces as you remove them.

Examine your furniture carefully for possible problem areas before you start.

✄ Look at all sides, including the bottom.

✄ Are any springs popping out through the upholstery or the dust cover on the bottom? If so, the piece probably needs interior repairs in addition to a new cover.

✄ Sit on the piece. Is it comfortable? Is the seat too firm or too soft? You might want to consider a different quantity or type of stuffing in the deck or a different interior construction for loose seat and or back cushions.

Place the furniture on the horses. As you strip, turn the piece in any direction necessary to give yourself comfortable access to the area you're stripping.

To strip, use pincers to loosen edges and a claw tool and hammer to remove tacks and staples. Loosen, pry away, and remove the old fabric and the other materials from the frame. If there's hand sewing, use small scissors or a utility knife to cut the stitches. You'll see that the allowances are either folded under the cover section or wrapped onto the adjacent surface of the frame. If tacking strips were used, they'll come off attached to the edges they finish along with the underlying padding. ▷

If your furniture is trimmed with gimp, braid, decorative nails, or other applied embellishment, remove them now. Any trim inserted between the pieces of the cover, such as welting, will be removed when you strip the adjacent pieces.

stripping the old fabric

Removing the First Piece

On almost any piece of furniture, the dust cover is the first piece to remove. Remove it, exposing the bottom webbing, frame rails, and cover edges. ▽

TIPS FROM THE PROS

✄Chairs and benches that have drop-in or slip-seats often have no dust cover. This is also true of furniture with elasticized webbing instead of jute webbing and springs.

Marking for Future Reference

Before you do anything else, cross-mark critical alignment and match points on the cover and frame, which will be important when you position the new cover (refer to photo 3, page 114). Using tailor's wax chalk or a permanent marker so the marks will be durable, draw a short line perpendicular to and across seams, across tacked joining, and across the edge of the fabric onto the frame. Mark right across any welting.

✄On one half of the cover (either the right or left side), cross-mark any seamlines, such as a deck seam, fascia, or boxing seams. Mark the midpoint of the seam and any points where other seams, tacked joins, or frame members intersect it. If the seam is curved, mark several points on the curve.

✄Cross-mark the midpoint on the top of the back and on all bottom edges. If there's a skirt or border, mark the midpoints on each tacked joining, plus any front, back, or side intersections, including fascias, vertical boxing, and pleats.

✄Mark the midpoints on the underside of the bottom rails and on any fabric allowances tacked to them.

✄Later, as you strip other pieces, continue to cross-mark their midpoints onto the frame as it becomes exposed.

Removing the Skirt

If your furniture has a skirt, remove it next. Fold up the skirt toward the body of the furniture to reveal the cut edges of the fabric and the tacks and tacking strips. Remove the tacks and tacking strips, then the skirt, and finally the welting.

✄If the skirt has illusory pleats, remove the backdrops first and then the tacks and tacking strips, skirt panels, and welting.

stripping other styles of furniture

If you're stripping a wing chair that has a flat-top arm, you'll find the flat top is sewn to the inside arm. Strip the flat top and inside arm off together, in the manner described for removing the fascia and inside arm on page 46.

If you're stripping a piece of furniture that has an applied fascia, remove the fascia after its bottom edge becomes accessible. Likewise, remove a border or vertical boxing section after its bottom edge becomes accessible.

If you're stripping a sofa bed, unscrew and detach the outside back and mattress frame after removing the dust cover, and then proceed with the stripping.

THE STRIPPING ORDER

Use the order given below as a general guide for stripping any piece of furniture. Depending upon the style of the piece you're redoing, you may encounter fewer, more, or different elements—just remember to work from the top layer down. Be sure to remove the applied trim, dust cover, and skirt, if there is one, first.

Outside Back
✂ Welting from bottom edge of entire chair.
✂ Bottom edge from back rail first, then side edges from back posts, top edge from the top rail last.
✂ Padding layer below outside back if it didn't come off with the back cover.
✂ Welting across top of back rail and along back posts. (Cut through welting at any point to make removal easier.)
✂ Burlap from outside back. △

Outside Wing/Outside Arm
✂ Outside wing/arm from back posts, wing rail, and post; front edges of outside arm along fascia and vertical scroll post; bottom edge on side rail and edge underneath horizontal scroll of arm.
✂ Padding under outside wing/outside arm.
✂ Burlap from outside wing/outside arm.

Inside Back
✂ Side edges along back posts, then top edge on top rail and bottom edge on bottom rail.
✂ If necessary, padding and stuffing under inside back.

Inside Wing
✂ Back edges on back post, front edge along wing rail and post, bottom edge over top inside edge of inside arm.
✂ If necessary, padding and stuffing under inside wing. ▽

TIPS FROM THE PROS
✂ If you find a muslin liner under the padding, chances are you can leave it and the stuffing beneath in place. If you must strip them, first remove the entire cover and padding, and then cross-mark and remove the liner and underlying layers.

Inside Arm and Fascia

✂ Welting behind vertical scroll and on outside of fascia.

✂ Back edge along back post, front edge together with sewn-on fascia, top edge under scroll of arm, bottom edge on side rail. ▽

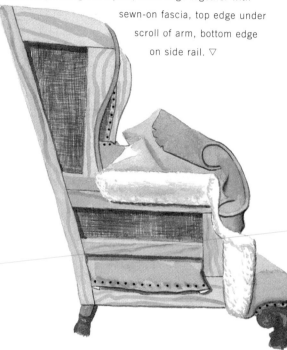

✂ If necessary, padding and stuffing under inside arm and fascia. ▽

✂ If your fascia is applied, remove it with its welting before stripping the inside arm.

✂ Separate the fascia, adjoining welting, and inside arm. ▷

Deck or Seat

✂ Lip edge on front and side rails, back edge of deck on back rail, and sides of deck on side rails.

✂ If necessary, padding and stuffing under deck and lip.

✂ Fox edging on front edge of lip.

Burlap

✂ If you stripped the stuffing and padding from the inside back, inside wings, and inside arms, remove all the inside burlap at one time.

TIPS FROM THE PROS

✂ Burlap becomes brittle with age. You should replace it on the outside sections even if your chair is fairly new and you're reupholstering it for cosmetic reasons only.

✂ Don't press the folds, creases, pleats, or seamlines out of the old cover pieces. Keep them just as they came off the furniture.

Loose Cushions

✂ If you haven't already done so, cross-mark the seams at the center of each side and at all corners.

✂ Unzip the cushion cover and remove the inside cushion. Turn the cover wrong side out and separate all the pieces.

repairing the innards

Once you've stripped your furniture, you'll have access to the frame, webbing, and/or springs and will be able to judge their condition and assess whether you can make any needed repairs yourself or should turn to a professional. For best results you should leave complicated repairs such as completely retying springs to an experienced hand, but there are many repairs you can do easily. If you plan to repair or refinish the frame, do so before making any other repairs.

REPLACING JUTE WEBBING

You can replace webbing yourself as long as it doesn't support springs, which is common on pad- or slip-seats and on some backs, wings, and arms, where the webbing is stretched across an open frame and layered directly with the burlap, stuffing, and other materials.

To replace webbing on a seat, follow the steps below. Use the same process for vertical areas, but work from bottom to top and omit the horizontal webbing from arms or wings. To learn how to slip-tack and tack, refer to pages 57–61.

1 Strip the furniture, including the old webbing.

2 With the cut edge extending 1" beyond the back edge, place a new strip of webbing from back to front across the frame; center the webbing on the center marks. Tack with four tacks. ▽

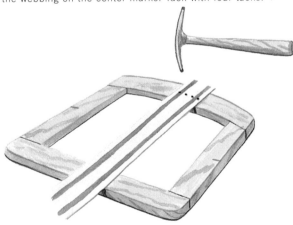

3 Fold the cut end of the webbing back over itself and tack again three times, between the previous tacks.

4 Pull the webbing tightly across the frame with one hand and insert the webbing stretcher, teeth upward, into the webbing. Insert the stretcher just far enough from the frame so that when you press the handle down and out, the top of the stretcher pushes against the frame edge, thus increasing the tension on the webbing. ▽

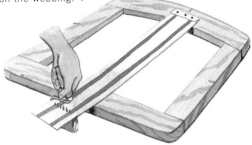

5 Keeping pressure on the stretcher so the webbing is as tight as possible, tack the webbing to the front of the frame.

6 Cut the webbing 1" beyond the frame, fold the cut end back over itself, and tack again three times as before.

7 In the same manner place additional strips of webbing parallel to the first one, spacing them 1"–2" apart.

8 To place webbing across the seat, begin at the center as before, but weave the cut end over and under alternate strips before tacking to the far side. Then stretch the webbing and tack to the near side. Repeat to weave additional strips of webbing parallel to the first, alternating the over–under sequence. ▽

TIPS FROM THE PROS

✂ To test the webbing tension, tap it with the tack hammer. The head should bounce off the surface.

repairing the innards

REINFORCING EXISTING WEBBING

In furniture with springs, it's possible to reinforce old, dried-out webbing that has lost its bounce. Do this only if the coil springs are in good condition and still securely attached to the webbing.

1 Turn the furniture upside down. Position a strip of webbing from back to front and slightly off center over the old webbing. Attach it as described in step 2 on the previous page. ▽

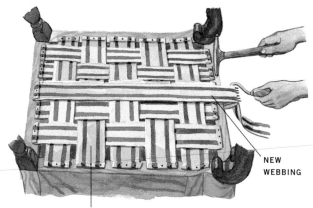

NEW WEBBING

OLD WEBBING

2 Following steps 3–8 on the previous page, weave a new webbing base; place each new strip slightly off center of the one it covers.

✂ To fit a strip of new webbing around a leg, slip-tack it to the frame close to the leg, then chalk the position of the leg on the webbing, and slash as shown. ▽

✂ Tack the webbing to the frame on each side of the leg in the usual tack-fold-tack method. ▽

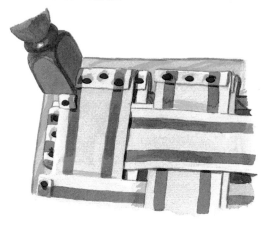

REPLACING ELASTIC WEBBING

New elastic webbing and the clamps that hold it on the furniture can be purchased from your supplier. When you replace them, duplicate the original arrangement.

REATTACHING COIL SPRINGS

If your furniture has coil springs, check their condition once you've stripped the upholstery. If the spring twine has popped loose from the frame or has broken between the springs in a couple of locations, you can easily reattach and repair these. However, if the twine is weak, broken, or loose overall, you should ask a professional to retie the springs. The tension applied as the springs are tied together creates the contoured shape of the seat, back, or arm they support—you might think patience is all that's required, but creating the proper tension is an art that an apprentice upholsterer takes months to master.

Knots

A variety of knots is used to anchor the springs to the webbing, to knot and yoke springs together, and to start and stop the tying process. These knots can also be used for simple repairs on coil and zigzag springs. Work from the inside of the frame so you can control the location of the springs. Some knots must be stitched through the webbing, so thread the twine through a long needle to begin with, and you'll be ready to stitch when required. A double-pointed straight needle will make this process easier than a single-pointed one.

Upholsterer's slip-knot: Use this knot to anchor the bottom ring of a coil spring to the webbing. On each coil make three evenly spaced knots. Leave about 6" of loose twine at each end when beginning or ending a length of twine. Pass the needle down and up through the webbing and wrap the knot as shown, then pull it taut. If you're reattaching more than one coil, work in a logical order from one to the next. ▽

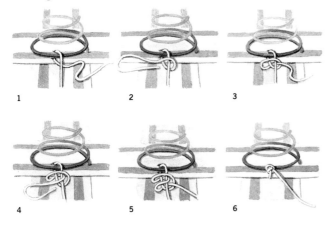

Overhand knot: Use this double knot to end off the twine when the slip-knots are complete. Loop the twine over itself as shown, pull taut against the slip-knot, and repeat. ▽

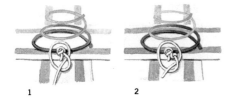

Twin-tack cloverleaf: Use this faux knot to anchor the ends of the spring twine to the rails before and after the springs are tied together with clove hitches *(right)*. It is used with both coil and zigzag springs.

✂To anchor the twine before tying the springs, place two slip-tacks $1/2$" apart on the rail and wrap as shown, then drive the tacks into the rail. ▽

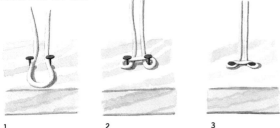

✂To secure the twine after tying the springs, place two slip-tacks $1/2$" apart on the rail and wrap as shown, then drive the tacks into the rail. ▽

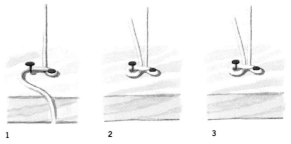

Clove hitch: Use this knot to yoke one spring—coil or zigzag—to another. After the hitch is made on one spring, carry the twine over to the next spring and make another clove hitch. In repairing and retying, duplicate the original tension to maintain the overall contour or plane of the surface. Wrap the twine as shown. ▽

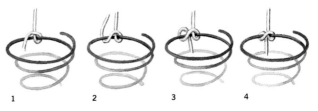

REATTACHING ZIGZAG SPRINGS

Zigzag springs can generally be reused. If for some reason you must replace them, measure the seat frame from the front outside edge to the back outside edge and cut the zigzag springs $1 1/2$"–2" longer than this dimension. Webbing isn't used under zigzag springs.

✂If the clamps that hold zigzag springs to the frame are bent or loose, replace or reattach them.

✂If there are ties between the springs, replace them if they're damaged. Anchor the twine to each side of the frame with a twin-tack cloverleaf and tie the springs together using clove hitches *(above)*; move in a zigzag fashion from one spring to the next.

✂If there are metal helical coils between the springs, reinstall them as they were originally attached if they've come loose.

repairing the innards

REPLACING BURLAP

Burlap becomes dry and brittle with age, so if you've removed the layers above it, remove and replace it. If you need to repair springs or the furniture frame, you'll have to remove the burlap first and then replace it when you're satisfied that the frame, webbing, and springs are in good condition.

If you're able to leave existing stuffing and padding on the inside vertical sections of your furniture, reinforce the burlap that supports them by tacking webbing behind it. Working from the outside of the frame, tack the webbing to the bottom face of the top rail of each section, pull it as taut as possible with your hands, and tack to the top face of the bottom rail or liner. You'll see photographs of reinforced burlap on page 115.

You can apply burlap section by section as you reupholster or all at once when you begin. If applying it all at once, attach a separate piece to each section; if you cover adjacent sections with one piece of burlap, you won't be able to pull through the cover tacking allowances later.

Cut each piece of burlap as a rectangle, tack it to the frame, and then trim it to follow the frame contours. Fold the edges back onto themselves and tack again for reinforcement (see page 58).

REPLACING STUFFING AND PADDING

You should always replace the padding on the outside sections of your furniture. If you need to replace the stuffing and padding on the inside sections, do so section by section as you reupholster. Refer to Putting on the Cover, pages 77–111, to learn when and how to install them.

With the exception of foam, stuffing materials are usually reusable. Remove and replace all foam, using the same thickness. Select a firm density for seats and a soft density for other locations.

If your furniture is of very fine quality, you're likely to find a layer of muslin under the padding and a second layer of padding under the muslin. If at all possible, leave these layers on the furniture; it isn't easy to duplicate their contours.

Whether you reuse or replace them, be sure to add a layer of polyester padding over them; it's stable and durable, it retains its loft over time, and the cover will sit smoothly over it.

Securing Stuffing and Padding to the Frame

When you position unstable stuffings and paddings, such as horsehair and cotton batting, hold the material firmly against the frame without tugging; stress will cause the fibers to separate. When you position stable stuffings and paddings, such as foam, rubberized horsehair, and polyester padding, you can pull and stretch them if necessary. There's no need to attach stuffing; it will be held in place by the tension of the layers on top of it. Slip-tack or permanently tack padding to the frame as necessary. Refer to Putting on the Cover, pages 77–111, for more specific information.

REPLACING FOX EDGING

If you found fox edging (also called an *edge roll*) next to the burlap, it can be reused if it's in good condition, or you can replace it. Position it where it was along the frame edge with the roll facing out and the flange facing in.

✄Unless you're applying fox edging over a seat with an edgewire, tack the flange to the frame with carpenter's nails.

✄Because there's no wood frame on the top edge of an edgewire, you must whipstitch the fox edging flange to the burlap covering the seat or deck and blanket-stitch the rolled edge to the drop of the lip (refer to pages 67 and 69). Use a 6" curved needle and heavy polyester thread to sew. ▷

cutting the new cover

Professional upholsterers cut as they go, and you're advised to do the same. You'll layer and cover the furniture one section at a time, and there are many variables that can pop up as you work. If you wait to cut each piece until you're ready for it, you'll have the flexibility to cut the piece a little larger or to alter the position of a motif, should this be necessary.

When you cut the new cover, you'll cut some pieces by following the measurements on your cutting list and others by using the old cover as a guide. For most furniture the majority of the cover pieces are tacked individually to the frame; you'll measure and mark their cutting outlines directly on the fabric. Check your notes from your stripping steps to see if any of the pieces were sewn together when you removed them. If so, note whether these are symmetrical or asymmetrical, because you'll handle the two differently. The methods to use in each situation are explained later in this section.

TIPS FROM THE PROS
✂Duplicate any cross-marks on both sides of the newly cut cover pieces. You'll never have to think about which side you'll be referring to. Use a nonpermanent marker on the right side.

GETTING STARTED
Before beginning to cut, examine the full length of your fabric. If you find flaws before you start, manufacturers will replace the yardage. If you find them after you've started cutting, too bad!

After examining the fabric, cut off a piece long enough to yield all the bias strips you'll need to make your welting (refer to page 40). On either the right or wrong side of the fabric, draw parallel chalk lines 1³/₄" apart along the bias. Use a 45-degree right-angle triangle to locate the first bias line, and then use a ruler to measure and mark the rest. ▽

Place the rest of your fabric right side up on your cutting table.

CUTTING PIECES THAT WILL BE APPLIED INDIVIDUALLY
Pieces that will be applied individually to the furniture should be cut as squares or rectangles following the dimensions marked on your cutting list; their curves and angles will be refined as you attach them. Refer to your cutting diagram to see how to align any pattern repeat or motif. Use a square and ruler and chalk to mark the cutting outlines on your fabric.

CUTTING PIECES THAT WILL BE SEWN TOGETHER
Most pieces that will be sewn together before they're placed on the furniture should be cut using the old cover as a pattern. The exception is pieces that will be joined with straight seams, such as the lip and deck. To be sure that you're adding the proper seam and tacking allowances, refer to your cutting list as you work.

Because this barrelback chair has several pieces—both symmetrical and asymmetrical—that are sewn together, we've chosen it to demonstrate this part of the cutting process.

✂The inside and outside backs are symmetrical; each has a seam allowance on all but its bottom edge, which has a wide tacking allowance.
✂The inside arm/outside arm wraps seamlessly around the face of the arm post and has an unusual asymmetrical shape; it has a seam allowance on all but the bottom edge.
✂Of the three shoulder pieces (the strips along the top), the center back shoulder is symmetrical, the side shoulders are asymmetrical. All have ¹/₂" seam allowances all around.
✂The seat is the only piece that would be cut as a rectangle and shaped as it is tacked to the frame. △

cutting the new cover

Cutting Symmetrical Pieces That Have Seams

Pieces such as the inside and outside back and center top shoulder of the barrel chair are symmetrical. To cut pieces like these, first fold the old cover piece in half lengthwise, wrong side out. Align the fold with the straight grain of the new fabric, placing it as necessary on a repeat or motif. Be sure to position the piece so as to allow the appropriate tacking allowance on any edges that won't be sewn together; measure from the crease on the old cover and mark the cutting line.

Cut out one half of the new cover piece: Follow the seam edge of the old cover, being sure to include a $1/2$" seam allowance from the creased seamline to the cut edge; also cut on the marked tacking allowance lines. ▽

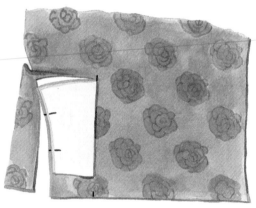

Along the cut edges of the new piece, transfer any cross-marks to the wrong and/or right sides. Remove the old cover piece. Fold the cut half of the new cover piece onto the uncut fabric along the center marks. ▽

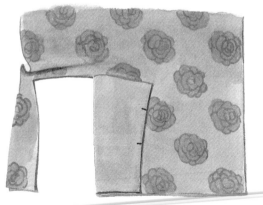

Cut out the second half of the new cover piece, using the first half as a pattern. Transfer the marks as before.

Cutting Asymmetrical Pieces That Have Seams

Pieces such as the wraparound inside arm/outside arm and the side top shoulder strips are asymmetrical. To cut pieces like these, place the old piece on top of the new fabric, both right side up. Be sure to position the piece so as to allow the appropriate tacking allowance on any edges that won't be sewn together; measure from the crease on the old cover and mark the cutting line.

Cut out the new cover piece: Follow the seam edge of the old cover, being sure to include a $1/2$" seam allowance from the creased seamline to the cut edge; also cut on the marked tacking allowance lines. Along the cut edges of the new piece, transfer any cross-marks to the right and wrong sides. ▽

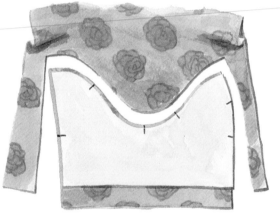

TIPS FROM THE PROS

✄For any piece of furniture with a loose seat cushion, cut the deck and lip as rectangles, referring to your chart. Add a 2" seam allowance on their adjacent edges to ensure you've enough to manipulate around any posts.

✄For any piece of furniture with a sewn-on fascia, cut the inside arm and fascia using the old cover as a guide. They're asymmetrical. Do the same for any fascia with sewn-on welting.

✄Be sure to check the fit of any cushions before cutting their new covers. See pages 78 and 95 for more information.

CUTTING SUPPORTING MATERIALS

Cut new layers of burlap, foam, stuffing, padding, and muslin as you need them. Cut these materials as rectangles, following the cutting dimensions recorded on your chart. The pieces will be shaped and trimmed as you place them on the furniture.

cutting pleated skirts and their linings

A skirt is a panel or series of panels arranged around the furniture to hide the legs. On large furniture pieces the skirts can contain two or more pleats on any side.

In traditional upholstery the pleats in a skirt are illusory, with separate top and backdrop (the inside of the pleat) panels. This is because the fabrics don't hold creases well, especially once they've been lined for extra body; a crisp, pleated effect is more successful when the panels are individually interfaced and lined. However, some contempory designs work well with softer skirts pleated from one length of fabric.

MEASURING FOR A PLEATED SKIRT

Measure the width on the front, back, and one side of the furniture just below the front lip (or box) beneath the seat or cushion. Measure the depth from the bottom of the front lip, or the bottom of the welting cord attached there, to the floor. Measure the width of each panel individually; the depth should be the same for all. ▽

✄The standard finished width for backdrops is 9"; don't measure for them, just count how many you'll need.

✄If your furniture is long with one wide skirt panel from corner to corner and you're using a vertically run fabric, plan to sew three panels of fabric together as you did for the body of the furniture. For furniture with tight seat upholstery, align the skirt seams with the seams on the seat and outside back. For furniture with loose cushions, align the seams with the cushion junctions. The lining may also need seams.

CUTTING THE SKIRT

To the measurements for each skirt and backdrop panel, add 3" at each end to allow for a 2¹/₂" self-facing and a ¹/₂" seam allowance. Add a ¹/₂" seam allowance on both the top and bottom.

Cut out the skirt panels, matching the fabric pattern to the lip or boxing strip as necessary; match each backdrop to the pattern of the panels on top of it. At each end of each piece, press 3" to the wrong side for the self-facing and seam allowance.

Cutting the Interfacing and Lining

Each piece of the skirt should be interfaced with a very stiff woven or nonwoven fabric. Interfacing is cut to the finished dimensions of the skirt panels and backdrops. Cut an interfacing for each piece, omitting the facing and seam allowances.

Each piece of the skirt should be lined. The lining will be sewn to the vertical cut edges of the self-facings, so for each piece, you can omit the width of both the facings from the lining width; you'll still need the ¹/₂" seam allowance on each edge. Cut a lining for each piece, making it the same depth but 5" (twice the 2¹/₂" self-facing) narrower. ▽

TIPS FROM THE PROS

✄When discussing long, narrow pieces such as skirt panels, it can be difficult to understand what is meant by the terms *length* and *width;* so use *depth* to refer to the top-to-bottom measurement and *width* to refer to the side-to-side measurement.

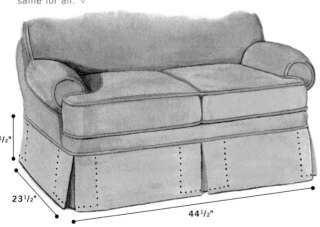

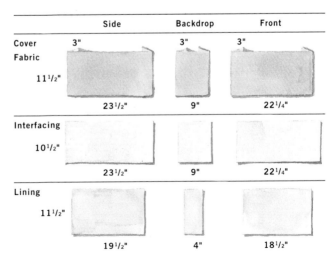

		Side	Backdrop	Front
Cover Fabric	11¹/₂"	3" · 23¹/₂"	3" · 9"	3" · 22¹/₄"
Interfacing	10¹/₂"	23¹/₂"	9"	22¹/₄"
Lining	11¹/₂"	19¹/₂"	4"	18¹/₂"

basic construction techniques

As you reupholster your furniture, you'll cut the materials to their final shape; secure them to the frame; stretch, wrap, fold, or pleat them to fit; possibly sew some of the pieces together; and apply trim. In this chapter you'll learn the various techniques you'll employ. The order in which they're explained has no bearing on the order in which you'll use these techniques, so familiarize yourself with all of them before beginning your project. Once you set to work, you'll use them alone and in various combinations.

CUTS FOR FITTING

You'll refine the shape of each piece of the inner materials and cover fabric as you put it on the furniture, cutting it wherever necessary so it fits smoothly with a minimum of bulk around the frame. To do this you'll use specific cutting techniques, each of which allows you to contour the shape of the materials in a different way and ensures that you maintain the proper tacking allowances as you work. Manipulating Fabric, pages 61–65, explains how you handle the fabric and finish the cut edges in different situations.

Following are the cuts you'll use. General methods for how to make each are given, along with examples for when you might use it. Before you make any fitting cuts, position the fabric (or other material) on the furniture and secure with pin-tacking and/or slip-tacking. Whenever possible, fold the allowance back onto the fabric, away from the point being slashed to, so you can see the element you're cutting toward. Always refer to the pieces of your old cover as you work; you should duplicate the type of cuts you see in each. The name of a cut often identifies its shape or tells what it looks like.

Clipping

A clip is a short, straight cut within a seam allowance or within the remains of a trimmed tacking allowance. Clips release tension where planes intersect; they also permit pieces with unlike shapes to spread and turn so they can be sewn or tacked together. Often you'll make a series of clips along a curved edge.
✂Use clips along the concave curve on an inside arm so it can be sewn to the convex edge of a fascia; on welting seam allowance, when the allowance must turn an outside corner or follow a convex curve on a cushion. See illustration *above right*.

Notching

A notch is a short, V-shape cut that removes a portion of the allowance. Notches eliminate bulk on curves or inside corners.
✂Use notches on welting seam allowance, when the allowance must turn an inside corner on a cushion; on the flange of fox edging when it turns around a T-shape deck; at any area where an allowance must condense after the fabric turns back along a convex curve, as on the inside arm edge of a fascia. ▽

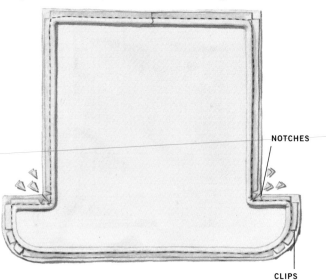

NOTCHES

CLIPS

Slashing

A slash is a long, straight cut made in a tacking allowance. Slashes allow the fabric to spread; they release tension where planes intersect, permitting the fabric to change direction. Once slashed the fabric can be manipulated so it lies smoothly around intersecting parts of the furniture or tacked to the frame.
✂Use slashes at curved areas of a fabric edge, such as on the front edge of an inside wing; on the bottom allowance of an outside cover piece at the inner corner of each leg. ▽

Diagonal Corner Cut

A diagonal corner cut is a slash along the bias from the point of an outside corner toward the interior of a piece. It permits the fabric to lie smoothly along two adjacent faces of a square-edged post.

✄ Use a diagonal corner cut to fit fabric around a post at the front or back seat corners. Slip-tack the fabric to the seat rails to within a couple of inches of the post. Fold the corner diagonally back onto the seat and slash up to the post corner. ▽

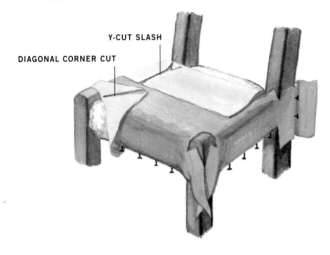

Y-CUT SLASH

DIAGONAL CORNER CUT

If your furniture has an exposed post, as shown above, unfold the fabric, leaning it against the post, and clip the slash edge at the side front and side back corners of the post. This will enable you to manipulate one section of the allowance at a time so you achieve a snug fit.

Y-cut Slash

A Y-cut slash is a long, straight slash with a V-shape cut at the inner end. This slash permits the fabric to separate and lie smoothly along three sides of a square-edge post or arm. The space across the open end of the Y equals the width of the post or other element being fitted.

✄ Use a Y-cut slash to fit fabric around a post at the back of a seat; at an arm post that joins the side or front of a seat; at an arm rail where it joins a back. Fold the fabric back to expose the post. Aim the slash toward the center of the post, stop short of the post, and make a short diagonal cut toward each edge of the post. △

If you're fitting the fabric around an exposed post, as shown at left, unfold the fabric, leaning it against the post, and clip the slash edge at each corner of the post at the seat edge, which will enable you to manipulate one section of the allowance at a time so you achieve a snug fit. (Handle the cuts around an arm rail in the same manner, clipping the inside back at each corner of the rail at the front edge.) ▽

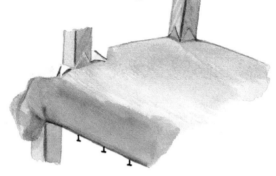

Once they've been clipped at the seat edge, the edges of the Y-cut slash will meet on the outside of the seat below the post. ▽

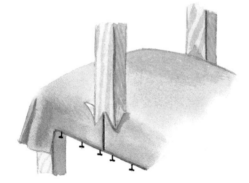

To maintain the tension on the fabric while you're making slip-tacking or additional cuts, you can slip-tack it temporarily to any nearby unfinished face of the frame.

At back seat corners you may have a choice between making a diagonal corner cut or a Y-cut—often either will work. The Y-cut is easier to make because you fold the back allowance forward across the seat and can see both posts at once. Slip-tack the back allowance after making both Y-cuts.

The diagonal corner cut is a better choice for the front corners because you make it with the allowance slip-tacked to the rails, thus assuring the position of the fabric on the seat.

Radiating Slashes

Radiating slashes are similar to Y-cut slashes or diagonal corner cuts, except they've multiple clips in the allowance at the inside end of the slash, making it possible to fit the fabric tightly around a curve.

✂ Use radiating slashes to fit the fabric around a round post or arm. Fold the fabric back to expose the post. Aim the slash toward the center of the post and cut up to the post. ▽

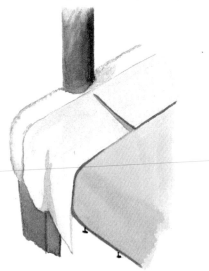

Unfold the fabric and place the edge of the slash vertically against the post. With your finger smooth the fabric against the post, away from the tip of the slash, until you feel the tension in the fabric. Clip the fabric horizontally about 1" above the seat and then clip down, toward the seat, releasing the tension. Repeat this process around the post, clipping the allowance on both edges of the first slash. (Handle the cuts around an arm rail in the same manner, clipping the inside back around the rail.) ▽

TIPS FROM THE PROS

✂ If a cover piece was cut as a rectangle and a portion of it must be cut away to enable it to fit around a post or arm, you'll cut right through the tacking allowance and into the body of the piece so you can give the piece its final shape; you'll probably use a combination of different slashes and cuts to do this.

✂ Unclear about the difference between notches and clips? If the allowance pleats onto itself when you turn it to its final position, it should be notched to remove the excess bulk. If it binds when you try to manipulate it, it should be clipped so it spreads as needed.

✂ At corners a single clip or notch will suffice; at curves you'll need several.

✂ Never notch an allowance that will be inserted into a flexible tacking strip.

✂ Clip allowances that will be inserted into a flexible tacking strip only if necessary, then clip no closer than $1/2$" from the jaw.

✂ When making a slash or diagonal corner cut, place your hand under the allowance being slashed and let your finger mark the stopping point.

✂ Always slash shy of what you judge the stopping point to be. Push the cover down in place and check the length of the cut. If necessary, pull the corner out and cut further. It is better to go back and cut a little further than to cut too far at first and be sorry.

✂ Should you need to slash for exposed posts at both the front and back corners of the seat, slash for the back posts first; slip-tack the allowances as appropriate, smoothing the fabric over the seat; and then slash for the front posts.

SECURING FABRIC TO THE FRAME

In upholstery the fabrics are attached permanently to the furniture frame—at least until you decide to redo the upholstery again. This is true for some of the inner layers as well as the cover. Most pieces are attached individually. In some cases two or more pieces are sewn together and then attached. As you position and manipulate the fabrics, you'll often attach them temporarily before securing them for good, which allows you to refine their size, shape, and alignment. When securing loosely woven inner fabrics, you should reinforce their edges so they don't pull out under pressure.

Whether you're attaching the fabric temporarily or permanently, match the center marks on the fabric to those on the frame, and work from the center of each edge toward the ends or corners. Keep your eye on the lengthwise and crosswise fabric grain, they should stay perpendicular or parallel to the floor. Read Manipulating Fabric, pages 61–65, to learn more about handling the fabric as you work, and Putting on the Cover, pages 77–111, for more information about which type of tacking to use when.

Securing Fabrics Temporarily

Slip-tacking and pin-tacking are two ways to secure the fabric or other materials temporarily. If you need to make adjustments, you'll remove the temporary tacking, reposition the fabric, and tack temporarily again. When no further adjustments are needed, you'll tack the fabric permanently using one of the methods described later.

Slip-Tacking: Using a magnetic tack hammer, insert upholstery tacks through the fabric allowance and halfway into the wood, spacing them at 4" intervals. Alternatively, use a staple gun and staples. ▽

Pin-Tacking: Insert upholstery pins through the fabric allowance and into the seamline of the welting (which will already be installed on the frame) or into an inner layer of fabric or padding where there's no welting. If you'll be permanently tacking an edge with a flexible tacking strip, you'll pin-tack it first, leaving the cut edge free to turn into the strip. ▽

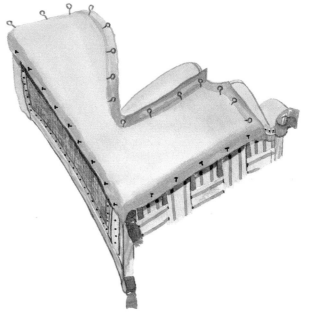

basic construction techniques

Securing Fabrics Permanently

After temporarily securing the fabric to the frame, making any necessary adjustments for smoothness and tightness, checking placement of motifs and repeats, and making fitting cuts, you'll be ready to secure it permanently. There are two tacking methods. The one you'll use most is **conventional tacking,** in which the tacks remain exposed until another layer of material covers them. **Blind-tacking** is used to finish as well as secure the fabric edge; the tacks are concealed inside the turned-under allowance. When blind-tacking you'll use one of three kinds of tacking strips to turn under the fabric edge; each type of strip has a specific purpose.

Conventional tacking: Use conventional tacking when the allowance will be covered by another layer of material or when the tacks form a decorative trim along the cover's edge.

Fill the spaces between the slip-tacks with several more tacks or staples, driving them all the way into the frame; also drive the slip-tacks all the way into the frame. If stapling remove any tack slip-tacks and replace with staples. Keep the fabric pressed firmly against the frame while you hammer with the mallet. If necessary, use your pincers to tug and hold the fabric taut. ▽

Reinforcing loosely woven edges: If you're installing a layer of loosely woven material, such as webbing or burlap, reinforce the cut ends or edges to ensure that they won't pull out from the tacks over time (see photo 6, page 115). First tack the fabric in the conventional manner, placing the tacks at least $3/4$" inside the edge of the frame. Trim the allowance 1" beyond the edge of the frame.

Fold the edge back over the tacks, flatten the fold by tapping with the mallet, and tack again. There should be a $1/2$" margin exposed at the edge of the frame. You'll use this area to attach the other layers of materials. ▽

TIPS FROM THE PROS

✄ Edge reinforcement is optional on a muslin liner used over padding or stuffing.

Blind-tacking with cardboard tacking strips: Use cardboard strips when blind-tacking a straight edge from the wrong side of the fabric, such as when securing the top edge of an outer arm, the bottom edge above a leg, the top edge inside an exposed frame, or the top edge of a skirt or boxing strip. There's no need to trim the tacking allowance. You'll usually use cardboard tacking strips to secure the first edge of a piece; that edge is likely to be horizontal.

To blind-tack with cardboard tacking strips, work as follows:

1 First, cut a piece of cardboard tacking strip the length of the edge to be tacked.

2 On the edge to be tacked, fold the allowance to the wrong side, and insert the tacking strip under the allowance, next to the fold.

3 Hold the fabric, right side out, over the furniture to check its position and alignment. If necessary, adjust the allowance vertically and the piece horizontally to align or position a motif.

4 At the center of the folded edge, hold the fabric in position with one hand. With the other hand reach under the fabric and flip it over so the wrong side is exposed. At the center tack the cardboard and the allowance to the frame.

5 Continue to tack the cardboard and allowance to the frame, stopping ½" from each side or end. As you tack, stretch the fabric as necessary. Repeatedly flip the fabric back and forth from the wrong to the right side to make sure you're achieving a straight, pucker-free line.

6 At each end trim the cardboard even with the frame edge, just inside any welting, or where it abuts another strip. ▽

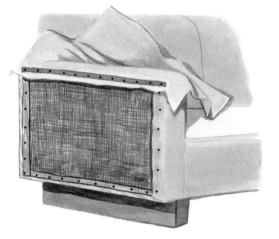

Blind-tacking with rigid metal tacking strips: Use rigid metal tacking strips when blind-tacking a straight, vertical edge from the right side of the fabric. They come 30" long and can be cut as necessary; if one is too short, simply butt two together. These strips are often used to secure the sides of an outside piece after its top edge has been secured with cardboard strips. Before tacking, permanently secure the top and bottom edges of the fabric (or any edges that won't be secured with the rigid metal strips).

To blind-tack using rigid metal tacking strips, work as follows:

1 Trim the side allowance 1" beyond the edge of the side welting.

2 Place the rigid metal strip under the top fold, aligning it inside the side welting. Mark the length of the side edge, less ¼", on the metal strip, remove it, and cut where marked.

3 Reinsert the rigid strip under the side, align its inside edge with the welting seamline, and point the teeth toward the fabric.

4 While holding the rigid strip firmly in the step 3 position with one hand, use the other hand to stretch and press the trimmed fabric edge over the strip and onto its teeth as shown. Work from the top to the bottom of the strip, stretching and puncturing a short section of the fabric at a time. ▷

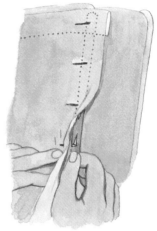

5 Using both hands, turn the rigid strip over so the teeth point toward the furniture.

6 Hold the strip against the welting. Check the folded edge of the fabric to make sure it's smooth. If necessary, flip the strip out again and adjust the fabric.

7 Working from top to bottom, use the mallet to hammer the rigid metal tacking strip into the frame. ▷

TIPS FROM THE PROS

✂ Rigid metal strips come with rounded ends. Always install the rounded end at the top of the furniture; the curve protects the top corner of the cover.

✂ If you're covering a rectangular outside arm, use a rigid metal tacking strip to finish the front edge after securing the top and back edges.

✂ You can also use a rigid metal tacking strip to secure the top fold of a mitered corner.

✂ Both rigid and flexible metal tacking strips are sometimes referred to as *tackless* methods for securing fabric.

Blind-tacking with flexible metal tacking strips: Flexible metal tacking strips can be shaped to follow almost any curve, so they're wonderfully versatile. Use them when blind-tacking any edge—straight or curved—on any outside cover piece. You can also use them to blind-tack the cover inside an exposed frame. While flexible strips look best inside a welted edge, they can also be used to finish some edges that may not be welted; for instance, on the top edge under a scrolled or a rolled back.

To blind-tack using flexible metal tacking strips, work as follows; if you're only securing one edge of the cover, omit the directions for turning the corner:

1 Cut a piece of flexible metal tacking strip the length of the edge you're finishing, plus a couple of extra inches.

2 With the toothed half of the jaw on top, place the flexible tacking strip over the welting seam allowance; butt the edge with the tabs and holes against the welting seam. Begin at the bottom corner of one side. Tack the lower end to the furniture.

3 Placing the edge snuggly against the welting, carry the flexible tacking strip up with one hand. With the other hand, tack it to the frame at $1/2$" intervals. ▽

TIPS FROM THE PROS
✂ Most professionals use a staple gun to attach flexible tacking metal strips to the frame. If you prefer tacks, insert them through the holes in the tabs.

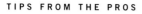

4 Continue to position and tack the flexible tacking strip along the side. When you reach the top, turn the corner and continue across the top and down the other side.

5 Close the jaw by pressing the toothed half of the strip over the tacked half with your fingers; leave a $1/8$" gap.

6 Place a layer of polyester padding over the section of the furniture you're covering. Tack it to the outside of the bottom rail. Smooth the padding up to the top, and tack it to the frame below the folded edge of the flexible strip. Smooth the padding out to each side; tack it to the frame next to the fold of the strip.

7 Trim the padding even with the flexible tacking strip jaw edge and any frame edges.

8 Position the upholstery fabric, matching center marks at the bottom and aligning any pattern as necessary. Slip-tack the bottom edge under the back rail.

9 Smooth the fabric over the furniture and pin-tack the top allowance and side allowances into the welting seamline along the flexible tacking strip jaw.

10 Use a regulator or a blunt, long needle to fold the allowance over the top of the ply grip, pushing it inside the open jaw. Begin on the top edge, working from the center to each corner. Remove the pin-tacks as you go, inserting a short portion of the allowance into the jaw at one time. Be sure the folded edge is smooth and pucker free. ▽

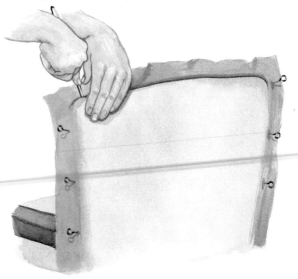

11 Trim the excess allowance; cut carefully along the flexible strip jaw. ▽

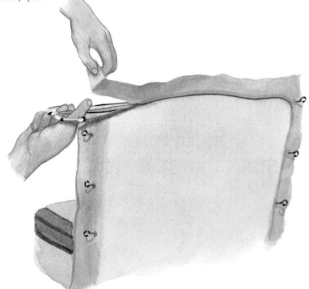

12 Use the regulator to push the edge of the allowance completely inside the flexible strip jaw, then close the jaw, using a mallet; leave the jaw open for about $1/2$" at each end.

13 Finish blind-tacking the sides in the same manner, then close the flexible strip where it was left open at the corners.

Securing Fabric with Needle and Thread

Although tacks, staples, and various tacking strips provide an easy way to secure fabrics, there's nothing wrong with sewing some pieces of the cover into position—after all, this is the way all upholsterers worked until fairly recently. In fact, there are times when you can't tack and may find it easier and faster to blindstitch by hand than to fit and remove the pieces and sew them by machine; for instance, when mitering a lip or securing a scrolled fascia. Or, if you can't locate tacking strips, you can sew the outside cover pieces to the welted edges. Refer to Sewing, pages 67–70, and the chapter Putting on the Cover.

MANIPULATING FABRIC

The cover fabric is the part of the upholstery that you notice. With the exception of trims, that's as it should be—the rest of the materials are intended to be hidden. When the fabric goes smoothly over the frame and innards, when every surface is snug and every pleat neat, the fabric has been well manipulated.

As you apply the fabric to your furniture, you'll handle it in several ways. You'll smooth it into position and stretch it taut before attaching it. It's probable that you'll fold your fabric into pleats or miters to eliminate or control it and make it conform to the shape it covers. Although only the cover fabric is visible on the finished reupholstery, the interior fabrics should be applied with the same care.

Learning to recognize the proper tension of the fabric as it lies over the furniture is key to successful reupholstery. As you gain experience you'll find your hands begin to work in a rhythmic manner and the cover will feel right when it's properly stretched. If you've no experience working with fabric, don't hesitate to practice by reupholstering a drop-seat (see page 66); you could even pin-tack some muslin over part of more complex furniture just to get a feel for the process.

While there are specific methods to follow for some fabric manipulations, the skill you'll need the most of is attentiveness. Every fabric behaves differently; use your eyes to see that your work looks right and your hands to judge that it feels right.

Placing the Fabric

Once you've cut a piece of fabric, you'll place it over the section of the chair it will cover so you can fit it, give it its final shape, and attach it. The exact way in which you position the fabric varies somewhat with the section of the furniture you're working on, but the same general principles apply throughout. Refer to Putting on the Cover, pages 77–111, for more specific information.

Place the fabric on the furniture, positioning it so that the allowances extend appropriately on all sides. If your fabric has a motif or repeating pattern, align it properly (refer to The Fabric Treatment, pages 32–35). Smooth the fabric from the center out in each direction. In the center of the piece, the vertical threads should be perpendicular to the floor (or the bottom rail), the crosswise threads parallel to it. (If you're positioning a seat, the threads should run straight from center front to center back and from side to side across the center.) After first smoothing the fabric, check the pattern alignment; reposition the fabric if necessary and smooth again.

basic construction techniques

Smoothing and Stretching

Once the placement is correct, you're ready to begin shaping and attaching the fabric. As you work you'll constantly smooth and stretch the fabric, cutting, shaping, and slip-tacking it as needed (if appropriate, use pin-tacks instead of slip-tacks while fitting, see page 57).

✂ To begin, slip-tack the center of the bottom edge, smooth the fabric up the center from bottom to top, pull taut, and slip-tack the center of the top edge.

✂ Then, smooth the fabric horizontally from the center of the piece to the midpoint of each side, pull taut, and slip-tack.

✂ Next, smooth and stretch each quarter-section of the piece from the center out and slip-tack at the corner. At this point the fabric will really begin to stretch and mold as it's being pulled along the bias. The fabric grain will no longer lie squarely over the frame; if you're working with a stripe or plaid, the lines will curve.

✂ Continue to smooth and stretch the fabric, placing additional slip-tacks along the edges. When covering a gently contoured section, like the back of this chair, you'll be able to stretch out the excess fabric along the edges without using pleats or tucks. ▽

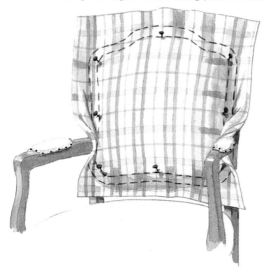

TIPS FROM THE PROS

✂ As you smooth, pull, and stretch the fabric between the first slip-tacks, keep an eye on the lengthwise and crosswise grain of the fabric. On symmetrical pieces keep them balanced from side to side. In asymmetrical sections keep the lengthwise grain perpendicular to the floor in the center of the piece; don't let it wander to one side.

✂ Always stretch from the center out, pulling the fabric taut over or onto the frame. Don't stretch the fabric along its cut edge.

✂ Don't try to ease in fullness that may appear in the fabric along the edges; it will never lie flat. Instead, keep pulling the fabric evenly in all directions until it hugs the contours of the inner layers and/or frame.

✂ If you see tension lines across the surface of the fabric, you've stretched it too tightly; release and adjust the slip-tacks as necessary.

Pleating

Pleats appear to be a decorative embellishment on some styles of furniture, and while they can indeed be handsome, they serve a practical purpose as well. You can control or eliminate excess fabric by pleating it. Pleats are especially useful when you're covering two adjacent surfaces and don't want a seam between them—they're often used to arrange the inside arm fabric in a fan pattern on the front of a scroll arm. Pleats can be shallow or deep; on upholstery, they're usually tapered.

The fan pleats on the face of a scroll always radiate from the inside of the scroll. Folding them evenly is a little tricky; you can refer to your old cover to see how they were spaced and angled, but every fabric will pleat differently, so you may need to make adjustments. Radiating pleats can face toward the center of the furniture or toward the side, but all the pleats on one scroll must face in the same direction. (If you're pleating side back or shoulder scrolls, the pleats will face toward the front or back of the furniture.) ▽

To form radiating pleats on the face of a scroll arm, first slip-tack the fabric to the arm, leaving it loose under the scroll at the front of the arm. Smooth the fabric onto the front of the arm, working up from the bottom of the furniture to the bottom of the scroll, and slip-tack the allowance on the side of the frame. Then form the pleats, cupping the fabric in your left hand and using a regulator to tuck radiating folds into the excess fabric as shown. ▽

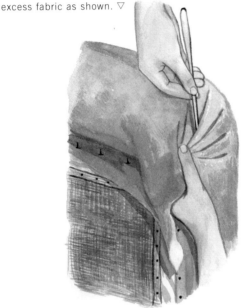

Begin by folding the fabric that wraps from the inside of the arm onto the arm front, not the fabric extending from under the scroll (the top edge of the inside arm); work toward the outside of the scroll. Face the pleats toward the side or center of the furniture.

To secure radiating pleats, tack the base (wider end) of each to the arm front; work from the bottom layer to the top and conceal each tack inside a pleat.

✂If the pleats face the center of the furniture, you can slip-tack them as you work, but to avoid repeatedly adjusting the slip-tacks, it's a good idea to experiment with the folds first to see how many you'll need and how deep they should be.

✂If the pleats face the side of the furniture, you must form them all before slip-tacking any. You won't be able to maintain the tension from the front of the arm if you try to form the outer pleats first.

When the pleats on the front of an arm are covered by an applied fascia, the fabric doesn't extend all the way across the face of the arm. The folds of these pleats probably won't meet under the applied fascia. You can fold all the pleats in one direction or change direction at the top of the arm. △

TIPS FROM THE PROS

✂If your new cover fabric is heavier than the old one, reduce the number of pleats and make each slightly deeper.

✂If your new cover fabric isn't as heavy as the old one, increase the number of pleats and make them shallower.

✂An odd number of pleats is always more pleasing to the eye than an even number.

Mitering

To box a corner without adding a second piece of fabric, you'll smooth and wrap the fabric onto the adjacent sides and fold the excess into one or two deep pleats. These pleats, or miters, are tacked to the furniture; in some instances you'll sew the folded edge closed. Depending upon the situation, miters can be vertical, horizontal, or diagonal.

You'll find miters at the front corners of T-shape decks or tight seats or any tight seat with a drop on three or more sides, including ottomans. You'll also find miters on the upper corners of tight backs.

basic construction techniques

Single miter: Position, smooth, and slip-tack the fabric in the manner appropriate to your furniture, leaving it free at the corner on the front rail. Wrap the side drop onto the front face of the rail and tack. Fold the front drop under as shown, aligning the crease with the vertical edge of the corner. ▽

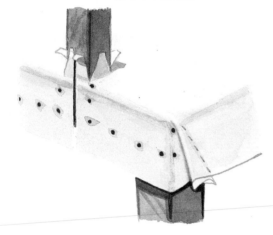

Trim the excess fabric from inside the miter. You can secure the fold with a rigid metal tacking strip or blindstitch it by hand. ▽

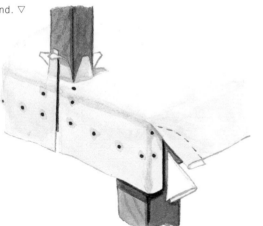

To fold a horizontal miter, such as on the top side edge of a T-shape deck, wrap the front drop around the corner to the side and fold the miter along the side top edge (see page 81).

Double miter: Position, smooth, and slip-tack the fabric in the manner appropriate to your furniture, leaving it free on both sides of the corner. Smooth the point of the corner fabric down, as shown, and tack to the rail on each side. Fold the excess fabric into a pleat on each side. ▽

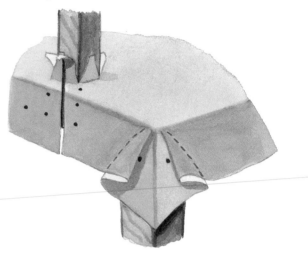

Smooth the drop down on each side, aligning the fold of each pleat with the vertical edge of the corner. ▽

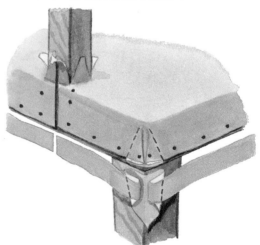

Finishing Slash Allowances

As you smooth, stretch, and tack the cover to your furniture, you'll probably slash the tacking allowances to fit some of the pieces around the arms and legs (refer to pages 54–56). As you slash, you'll create a number of smaller allowances, or flanges, which, because of their size or location, you won't be able to tack to the frame in the usual way. In some cases you won't tack them at all, but just tuck them out of the way. The flanges can be inserted between the inner layers and the frame, or between the cover and the padding beneath it. Refer to your stripping notes to see how your flanges should be finished.

✄To insert a flange between the inner layers and frame, use a regulator to gently roll down the flange until it rests flush against the frame; position the tip of the regulator in the middle of the flange, and don't apply pressure to the cut edges. Repeat to insert each adjacent flange. ▽

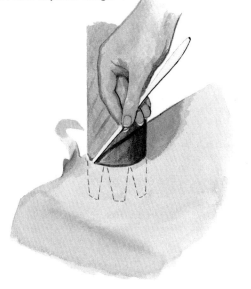

✄To insert a flange between the cover and padding, simply fold it under with your fingers while the cover is still loose.

✄If you're fitting the cover around an exposed arm or post, turn under the remaining edges of the slash before securing the drop. ▽

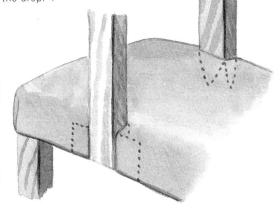

TIPS FROM THE PROS

✄The exposed cover fabric should fit smoothly around the post or arm. If it doesn't, pull the flanges out, clip a little bit deeper, and insert the flanges again.

✄If your deck has an edgewire, be sure to insert the flanges between the cover and padding. If you insert them against the frame, they'll work their way out as the edgewire moves up and down when the furniture is sat upon.

Finishing Welting Ends

Refer to page 74 to see how to trim and fold the fabric in order to finish the ends of welting, and then tack the welting allowance to the frame (see page 76). There's no need to restitch the bias over the cord before tacking.

upholstering a slip- or drop-seat

If you'd like to practice the skills needed for reupholstery before tackling a complicated piece of furniture, take a stab at recovering a simple drop-seat. Stuff the seat with foam, as explained here, or use several layers of stuffing covered with muslin and padding. Begin by stripping the seat.

When you reupholster the seat, you'll place a layer of muslin over the foam. As you stretch this liner onto the frame, it will compress the top edge of the foam, giving it a rounded profile. Before driving the slip-tacks all the way into the frame, check that the profile is pleasing.

1 If necessary, install new webbing. Tack new burlap over the webbing.

2 Measure the length and width of the seat frame. Add $1/2$" to each of these measurements; cut the foam to this size.

3 Put the foam on top of the frame. Measure the seat from bottom edge to bottom edge over the foam in each direction; add 4" to each dimension. Cut the muslin liner and upholstery fabric to these dimensions.

4 Place the liner on your worktable. Center the foam on top. With the bottom up, center the seat frame on top of the foam. ▽

5 At the center of the front and back, fold up the liner over the bottom rail. Pull taut and slip-tack. ▽

6 Repeat step 5 on the sides.

7 Working from the center to each corner and alternating between the front and back rail, continue to stretch and slip-tack the liner, tacking at 1" intervals. Repeat on the sides, stopping about $1^1/2$" from the corners.

8 At each corner fold the excess fabric into a miter, and then fold the tacking allowance onto the rail. Finish slip-tacking the allowance to the corner. Drive all tacks into the frame. ▷

TIPS FROM THE PROS

✂ You can use polyester batting instead of muslin for the liner. Trim away the excess at the corners, and glue the cut edges to the foam with spray-foam adhesive, and then finish tacking. Don't worry if the foam corners look a little higher than the sides at this stage; they'll be compressed by the upholstery fabric. ▷

11 Put the seat in the chair frame and check that the form is balanced. Remove the seat from the chair.

12 On the bottom of the frame, mark the center on each side. On the right side of the upholstery fabric, mark the center of each side. Place the fabric wrong side up. With the bottom up, center the padded frame on the fabric.

14 Matching the centers on each edge, stretch and slip-tack the cover fabric to the seat. Work as you did to apply the liner. Pleat a miter at each corner and slip-tack.

15 Turn the seat over. Check that all edges are smooth, the fabric tension even, and any pattern balanced. Turn the seat over again and drive all the tacks firmly into the frame.

17 To determine the size to cut the dust cover, place the upholstered seat right side up on the cambric and trace the perimeter of the seat. Cut out the dust cover $1/2$" outside the marked line. Place the seat bottom side up and center the cambric on it. Fold under $3/4$" on each edge. Tack the cover to the bottom of the frame through the folded allowance. ▽

TIPS FROM THE PROS

✂ Place a layer of polyester batting between the muslin and cover fabric.
✂ There's no need to add a dust cover if the seat has elastic webbing.

SEWING

Although most upholstery pieces are tacked rather than stitched to the furniture, you'll still do some sewing as you reupholster. In some cases you'll position a piece on the furniture and sew it in place by hand. Other times you'll sew two or more pieces together by machine before installing them on the furniture.

Hand-Sewing Stitches

For the most part you'll use hand sewing inside the furniture, not on the portions of the cover that show. You'll secure a two-piece deck seam to the stuffing and attach fox edging with hand stitches. Occasionally you'll sew a miter closed by hand. And, of course, inner cushions must be closed by hand.

Be sure to use the right needle and thread for the job; these are identified in Tools and Terms, pages 25–29, and in the following directions. Wear a thimble on the middle finger of your dominant hand; if you can get used to it, a thimble is much more comfortable than a hole poked in your finger by the needle end.

To knot the end of the thread, first wrap it around your index finger two to three times, then roll the wraps off your finger with your thumb, tugging on the length of thread with your other hand to tighten the knot. Insert the unknotted end of the thread into the eye of the needle.

After sewing, secure the thread with an upholsterer's slip-knot (refer to page 49).

The directions that follow are for right-handed people. If you're left-handed, reverse the left and right stitching directions and hold a mirror next to the illustrations to view them in reverse.

Blanket stitch: Use a blanket stitch to attach the rolled edge of fox edging to edges of furniture, such as on the lip of an edgewire deck or a scroll with a rolled edge. Work it from left to right, using a curved needle. To begin, take a tiny horizontal stitch, then insert the needle from top to bottom, passing the thread under the point of the needle as shown, and pull the needle through. Repeat, spacing the stitches at $^1/_2$" intervals. ▽

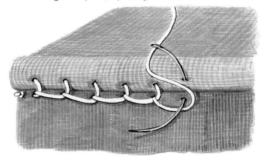

Hand basting: Use hand basting to temporarily sew two layers of fabric together to test the fit of the pieces or to align a motif or repeating pattern. Before basting, pin the pieces together on the seamline using dressmaker's pins; place the pins parallel or perpendicular to the cut edges. Work from right to left and remove the pins as you go. There's no need to end off basting with a slip-knot; you can make a few backstitches if you wish.

With your left hand, grasp the cut edges near the right end of the seam, placing your thumb on top of and index finger behind the seamline. Lift the fabric back and forth, passing it at $^1/_4$" intervals onto the point of the needle in your right hand. When the fabric builds up on the front half of the needle, shift the gathers off the back onto the thread, but don't pull the needle out of the fabric. Continue in this manner until reaching the end of the seam. ▽

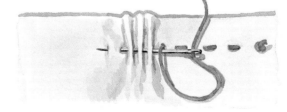

TIPS FROM THE PROS

✂Hand basting is easier to remove than machine basting, and the stitches are less likely to mar the fabric surface.

basic construction techniques

Lock stitch: Use a lock stitch to sew lapped seams on muslin liners as you install them on the furniture. It's very strong and can be used instead of tacking strips. Stand so the folded edge of the top layer faces away from you. Work from left to right, using a curved needle. To begin, take a tiny horizontal stitch, then insert the needle through the lower layer of fabric into the fold of the overlapping one. Wrap the thread around the needle as shown, push the wrap down the needle shaft to the fabric, and hold it there with your finger while you pull the needle all the way through. Repeat, spacing the stitches at $1/2$" intervals. ▽

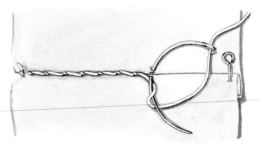

Running stitch: Use a running stitch to secure a seam allowance to the stuffing or padding so the cover fabric won't shift out of position. Also use it in areas where the allowance can't be tacked to the frame; for instance, the seam between the lip and deck. Use a curved needle and work in whichever direction is comfortable. Insert the needle through the seam allowance into the stuffing below. Bring the needle out about $1/2$" from where it was inserted. Repeat. ▽

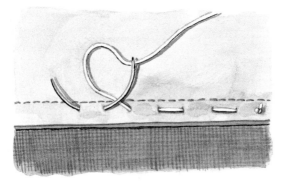

Slipstitch/Blindstitch: Use a slipstitch (also called a *blindstitch*) to sew an invisible seam from the right side of the fabric. Before rigid and flexible metal tacking strips were developed, upholsterers had no choice but to sew the outside cover seams by hand, and there are some instances where you may need or want to do the same.

You can slipstitch both lapped and butted seams. If working on a lapped seam, fold under the top seam allowance before you sew; if working on a butted seam, fold under both seam allowances. Use a curved needle. To reinforce the seam, begin and end the stitching a short distance from the end of the seam, working as follows.

To begin, insert the needle about 1" from the right end of the seam and, working to the right, make a $1/2$"-long stitch through the seamline of one piece and then another through the seamline of the other piece. Reverse your stitching direction and, working from right to left, complete the seam. Always insert the needle directly opposite the point at which it emerged. When you reach the end, reverse direction again and take two more stitches. ▽

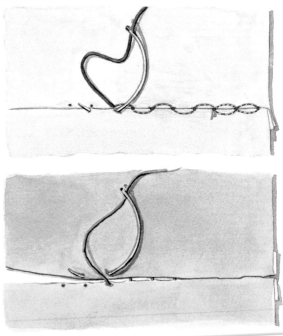

Spaced backstitch: Use the spaced backstitch to sew flat, decorative trim to the upholstery. If your thread is well matched to your trim, the stitches will be invisible. Work from right to left, using a curved needle. To begin, insert the needle from the wrong side of the trim, bringing it up near the top edge at least 1" inside the right cut end. Sew as shown, spacing the stitches about $^1/_4$" apart. ▽

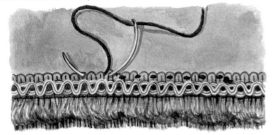

TIPS FROM THE PROS

✂ To finish the ends of the trim, turn them under. If they butt, slipstitch them together.

Whipstitch: Use a whipstitch to sew the flange of fox edging to a wire edge deck. Using a curved needle, work from left to right. To begin, pass the needle through the flange, then insert it from back to front through the deck into the flange, move to the right, and insert from back to front again, forming slanted stitches on top of the flange. Space the stitches at $^1/_4$"–$^3/_4$" intervals, as needed. ▽

TIPS FROM THE PROS

✂ After stuffing an inner cushion, you can use a whipstitch to close the opening. Sew with a conventional hand-sewing needle.

Machine Sewing

Although there are some types of furniture that can be reupholstered without using a sewing machine, for most you'll need your machine in order to make welting or loose cushion covers. Additionally, if your furniture has a two-piece deck, or a flat-top arm or a scroll with an inset fascia, you'll sew the pieces together and then install them as one unit. And, if the back or seat of your furniture is wider than your vertically run fabric, you'll have to sew several panels together before installing them.

Unless they join panels for a skirt or wide piece of furniture, cover seams are never pressed in upholstery. Instead, seam allowances are either oriented in one direction and hand-stitched to the furniture, such as to secure a deck seam to the stuffing; held in an open position by edgestitching or topstitching; or simply folded to one side as the pieces are placed on the furniture.

You may on occasion want to baste a seam before sewing it permanently. This can be particularly helpful if you're concerned about matching a difficult motif perfectly or if you have concave and convex curves fitting together, such as on a scroll arm with an inset fascia. You'll also find it easier to control the multiple fabric layers of welted cushion covers—especially in the corners—if you baste them first.

Following are directions for the machine-sewing techniques you'll need while reupholstering.

✂ Note that when sewing a straight piece such as welting or a boxing strip to a contoured piece, or when sewing two unlike curves, you'll have to clip the seam allowance of one piece or the other in order to fit them together smoothly. This is explained below, and you should refer to your stripped cover pieces to see where they were clipped.

basic construction techniques

Permanent seams: Adjust the stitch length to 8–10 stitches-per-inch; use fewer stitches per inch when sewing bulky fabrics. It's a good idea to make a test seam on scraps of fabric. Use dressmaker's pins to keep the fabric layers properly aligned while you sew.

Place the pieces to be joined right sides together. Matching any center or cross-marks, align the cut edges; pin or baste. Using a $1/2$" seam allowance, sew the pieces together; begin and end the seam with a few backstitches for reinforcement. ▷

Machine basting: Sew temporary seams in the same manner as permanent ones, but adjust the stitch length to 4–5 stitches-per-inch and omit the backstitching at each end. If it shows, remove the basting after sewing the seam permanently.

TIPS FROM THE PROS

✂ It isn't necessary to remove any machine basting you use to position welting. Even if you don't stitch precisely next to the cord, the basting will be concealed by the curve of the welt.

sewing the panels of a pleated skirt

If you're making a skirt with illusory pleats, the method for sewing each panel and backdrop is the same, regardless of its size. If any of the skirt panels are wider than your fabric, piece the cover and lining fabrics as necessary before beginning; press the seams open. Then sew each panel and backdrop as follows. Refer to page 53 to learn how to measure and cut out the skirt pieces.

1 With the right sides together and the cut edges aligned, pin and stitch the lining ends to the skirt panel ends, forming a ring. Press the seam allowances toward the lining.

2 Match the center marks on the top and bottom edges of the lining to those on the cover fabric. Pin and stitch the bottom seam. ▽

3 Turn the piece right side out. Match the center points on the top edge again and pin together. At each side edge press the facing foldlines. To keep the lining from peeking out on the finished skirt, press the bottom edge, rolling the seam about $1/16$" toward the lining.

4 Unpin the top edge of each panel and backdrop, and slide a corresponding interfacing piece inside each. The interfacing just floats inside the skirt; it will be held in place when the top edge of each panel is attached to the furniture.

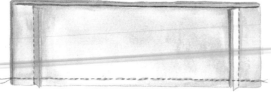

Edgestitching and topstitching: Once a seam has been stitched, use edgestitching or topstitching to hold the seam allowances open. The stitch length should be the same as that used for the seam. Always sew with the right side of the fabric facing up and the seam allowance underneath it; use your fingers to spread the seam allowance open as you feed the fabric into the machine.

✂Use edgestitching when you want the stitches to be inconspicuous. To edgestitch, stitch about $1/8$" from the seam, on each side of the seamline. ▽

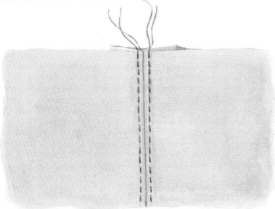

✂Use topstitching when you want the stitches to be apparent. To topstitch, stitch about $1/4$" from the seam, on each side of the seamline. ▽

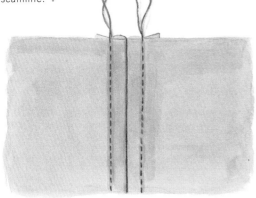

TIPS FROM THE PROS

✂To keep the allowances open on bulky fabrics, place the edgestitching or topstitching a little further from the seam.

Sewing outside corners: To turn a corner when attaching a straight piece, such as welting or a boxing strip, pin the straight piece to the other piece of fabric above the corner, with the right sides together and the cut edges aligned. At the corner, clip the seam allowance of the straight piece only right up to the seamline, pivot the straight piece around the corner, and continue pinning.

✂When you sew, place the pieces in the machine with the straight piece on top, stitch up to the corner, stop with the needle down, lift the presser foot, pivot the fabric, lower the presser foot, and continue stitching. ▽

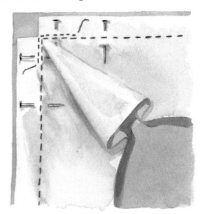

Sewing inside corners: To attach a straight piece, such as a boxing strip, to an inside corner, first clip the corner seam allowance right up to the seamline. Pin the piece with the corner to the straight piece, with the right sides together and the cut edges aligned, spreading the corner piece to fit the straight piece and keeping the cut edges aligned.

✂When you sew, place the pieces in the machine with the inside corner on top.

✂Sew welting to an inside corner in the same manner, but place the pieces in the machine with the welting on top. Read Attaching Welting, page 73, for more information. ▷

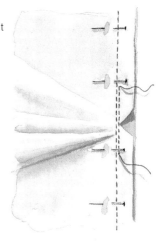

TIPS FROM THE PROS

✄ To reinforce the clipped allowance, staystitch it before clipping or sewing the pieces together. Simply sew along the seamline in the area to be clipped. If this area isn't obvious, such as around an inside corner, find it by pinning the pieces together or measuring, as appropriate; mark with chalk or pins.

✄ When sewing a piece that has both inside and outside corners, such as a T-shape cushion cover, sew with the straight piece on top and the piece with the corners on the bottom, and stitch the inside corner areas carefully, making sure you don't catch the spread fabric underneath in the seam. Alternatively, break the seam as necessary to sew each corner as described above. These seams will be easier to handle if you baste them first.

Sewing outside curves: To attach a straight piece such as welting or a boxing strip to an outside curve, pin the straight piece to the curved piece, with the right sides together and the cut edges aligned. At the curve, clip the seam allowance of the straight piece only right up to the seamline, clipping only as needed to spread the seam allowance around the curve.

✄ When you sew, place the pieces in the machine with the straight piece on top. ▽

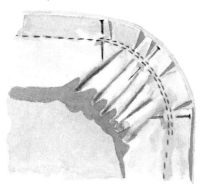

Sewing inside curves: To attach a straight piece such as a boxing strip to an inside curve, pin the piece with the curve to the straight piece, with the right sides together and the cut edges aligned. Clip the seam allowance of the curved piece only right up to the seamline, clipping only as needed to spread the seam alowance to fit the straight piece.

✄ When you sew, place the pieces in the machine with the curved piece on top. ▽

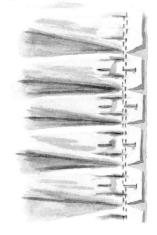

✄ Sew welting to an inside curve in the same manner, but place the pieces in the machine with the welting on top. Read Attaching Welting, page 73, for more information.

Sewing two unlike curves: To sew an inside curve to an outside curve, such as when sewing a scrolled fascia to an inside arm, handle the pieces in the same way you sew an inside curve to a straight piece, but spread the clipped seam allowance more so that it expands around the outside curve. In most cases, you'll have sewn welting to the curved edge of either the fascia or the inside arm before you have to sew the two pieces together.

Joining bias strips: To sew bias strips together so they'll be ready to turn into welting, place two strips right sides together, with the ends aligned as shown, and sew, making a permanent seam. Repeat to join all the strips. ▷

If your bias is striped or otherwise patterned, be sure to maintain the orientation of the pattern.

To save time, don't cut the thread after sewing two strips together. Instead, leave the needle down, fold up the free end of the top strip, and place it right side up in front of the presser foot. Top it with another strip, aligning the ends as before, and continue sewing. A short chain of stitches will form between each pair of strips; cut these after joining all the strips.

Making welting: Install the zipper foot on your machine, aligning it to the right of the needle. Adjust the stitch length to 4–5 stitches-per-inch. Place one end of the joined bias strip wrong side up, and center one end of the welting cord on top of it. Fold the bias over the cord, aligning the cut edges— there's no need to pin. Feed the cord and bias into the machine with the cord to the left of the needle and the seam allowance to the right under the presser foot. Sitch close to the cord, continuing to fold the bias over the cord as you sew. When you reach a seam on the bias strip, open it and continue sewing. ▽

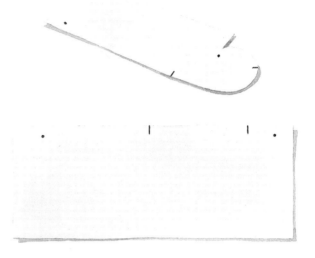

Attaching welting: To attach welting, pin it to the right side of the cover piece, aligning the cut edges. Position the zipper foot to the right of the needle and feed the piece into the machine, welting side up, with the cord to the left of the needle and the seam allowance to the right as before. Machine-baste the welting to the cover, stitching over the previous stitching on the welting.

If you're sewing welting around corners or curves, follow the clipping suggestions given at right.

Before sewing on the welting, mark the points where it should begin and end on the cover piece (or pieces) to which you'll be sewing it; mark them with a dot on both the wrong and right side of the fabric. The illustration below shows the cover for a flat-topped scroll arm. It's marked with dots for the welting and cross-marks that align with those on the inside arm cover beneath it. ▽

Sew the welting to one piece between the dots. When you position the second piece, be sure to align the match points. If appropriate, finish the ends of the welting as explained on the next page.

TIPS FROM THE PROS

It really isn't necessary to pin welting to an edge before you machine-baste it in place. In fact, the tension is likely to be better if you just hold the welting taut over the seamline while you sew; when you reach a corner, stop sewing with the needle down, clip the seam allowance as necessary, pivot, and continue sewing. You can pin the welting first, if you like, but don't be surprised if you need to adjust the pins as you sew.

To make it easier to fit the boxing to a loose cushion, machine-baste the welting to the cushion top and bottom— be sure the top and bottom are identical.

Trimming with Decorative Tacks

Insert decorative tacks using a special tack hammer with a soft plastic tip so you don't mar the tacks—or the cover or frame—should you misdirect your aim. Apply the tacks so they touch, or space them apart as necessary or desired. ▽

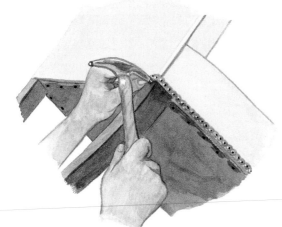

TIPS FROM THE PROS

✂If you're spacing the tacks apart, do your math first to find a workable interval. Although you might be able to remove a misaligned tack, it would probably be difficult to do so without damaging your cover and nearly impossible to conceal the hole piercing the fabric.

Tacking on Welting

Often a vertical piece of welting will butt against a horizontal piece. This occurs, for instance, when a single length of welting spans the top of the wings and back, crossing the welting on the sides of the outside back, or when a vertical welting meets the welting at the bottom edge of the furniture or the top of a skirt. When you encounter this, finish the end of the vertical piece before you tack it in place. If the welting encircles the furniture, such as around the bottom edge or above a skirt, lap and join the ends before tacking them (see page 74).

TIPS FROM THE PROS

✂As an alternative to finishing the bottom end of vertical welting, simply open the bias cover, snip out the excess cord, wrap the bias under the bottom rail, and tack to secure.

To tack welting to the frame, work as follows:

Positioning the end of the welting as appropriate, align the welting seam with the edge of the frame so the cord protrudes just beyond the edge and the seam allowance rests against the face of the frame. (If you're working on an interior joining, such as the intersection of the inside and outside arm, the cord should protrude onto the section already covered, as shown below.) Hold the allowance firmly against the frame with one hand and tack it in place. Guide the welting along the edge with one hand and continue to tack with the other. Clip or notch the welting seam allowance as necessary to contour it around corners and curves. ▽

IDENTIFYING THE FACES OF THE FRAME MEMBERS

Every frame member has four faces unless it's partially or completely round. The directions given later in this chapter often tell you to tack materials to a specific face of the frame, so it's a good idea to become familiar with them. Use the diagram below for quick reference.

The front face is the side that faces you when you face the chair front.

The back face is the side that faces away from you when you face the chair front.

The top face faces the ceiling.

The bottom face faces the floor.

The inside face faces the inside right or left side of the furniture—it's the side that faces you when you stand on the opposite side of the furniture.

The outside face faces the outside right or left side of the furniture—it's the side that faces you when you stand on the same side of the furniture.

Depending upon the configuration of the frame, some faces may not be exposed on all frame members—for instance, the front face of the arm rail often butts against the back face of the front rail or post. And some faces, such as those on the fascia and scrolls, merge into one another.

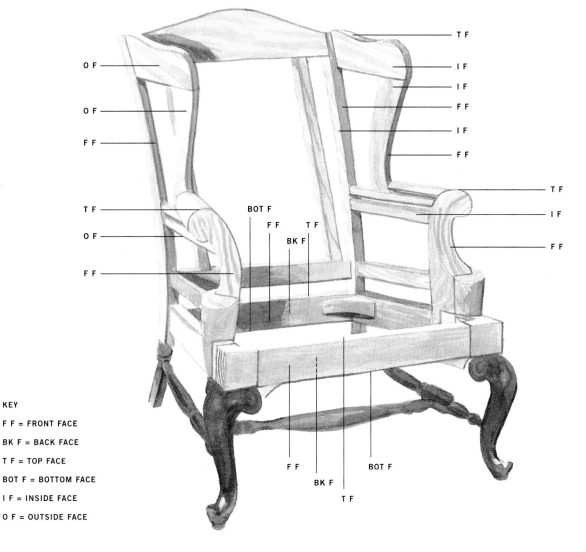

KEY

F F = FRONT FACE

BK F = BACK FACE

T F = TOP FACE

BOT F = BOTTOM FACE

I F = INSIDE FACE

O F = OUTSIDE FACE

THE DECK OR SEAT

Remember, the term *seat* is used when there are no loose seat cushions. The resting place for a loose seat cushion is called the *deck*. The two are covered differently—the deck has a seam across the front between the arms. Both can be T-shape or straight-sided. In this section the method for covering a T-shape deck is explained first, followed by that for covering a straight tight seat. If your furniture is a mix, read both parts and follow the pertinent information.

✄If your furniture has a T-shape seat or deck, you'll be mitering the front corners. If you wish to sew the miters by machine, fit the deck and lip, remove them, sew the miters, and reposition the deck/lip cover before securing it to the furniture.

Sewing the Deck

With the right sides together and centers matched, sew the lip cover to the deck cover.

Attaching the Deck

Lift the stuffing off the lip. Keep the deck/lip layered and place it over the deck with the wrong side of the lip facing up. Position the seamline just behind the front face of the arm post with the allowance facing forward. Using a running stitch, hand-sew the seam allowance to the burlap layer below (photo 7, page 115). If you like, you can pin-tack the center and ends of the seam through the burlap layer to secure while stitching.
✄Don't attach the deck at this time if you plan to sew the miters by machine. ▽

Attach the fox edging and reposition the stuffing on the lip. Roll forward the lip section of the cover right side up over the lip. Smooth the sections forward and backward enough to check the stuffing in the lip area. Lift up the lip and add more stuffing, if necessary, to make the front section about $1/2$" higher than the back. Then add a layer of padding over the lip stuffing (photo 8, page 116).

Slip-tack the front bottom allowance of the lip to the bottom face of the front rail, stopping several inches before the legs (photo 11, page 116).

TIPS FROM THE PROS

✄If you've sewn the deck/lip seam allowance to the deck, there's no real need to slip-tack the lip to the front rail at this time, but doing so will help to keep the lip out of the way while you work. If you haven't sewn the seam allowance to the deck, be sure to slip-tack now.

Arrange the back corners of the deck cover diagonally in front of the back posts. In each corner, cut a diagonal slash aimed toward the inside corner of the back post (photo 9, page 116). ▷

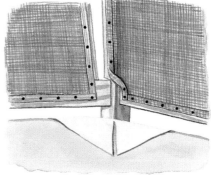

TIPS FROM THE PROS

✄Look at the slashes on your old cover. If they differ from those suggested here, follow those on the old cover.

Turn the left and right sides of the deck/lip cover onto the deck, wrong side up, so that a fold is created along each inside arm from the front to the back. Push the back allowance through to the outside between the deck and back liner. Stretch and slip-tack the back allowance to the bottom face of the back rail, stopping several inches away from the back legs.

On the deck section, slash through the side allowances of the cover; aim toward the back face of the arm post (photo 10, page 116). ▽

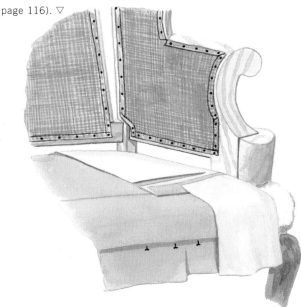

Pull the side allowances of the deck cover under the arm liners to the outside. Smooth and stretch the fabric and slip-tack the sides to the bottom face of the side rails, stopping several inches from the back and arm posts. Remove the slip-tacks as needed to adjust the length of the slashes just made, then slip-tack again.

At the front lip corners, turn the bottom allowance up over the front and side rails so it doesn't bind over the legs. Fit the cover tightly around the front and outside drop of the lip; above the exposed leg, slip-tack close to the folded edge through both layers into the ditch between the rails and leg.

Smooth and stretch the lip cover ends around the front corners along the side, and slip-tack the end allowance to the arm post.

Work along the top face of the lip to smooth the fabric over the padding and against the arm post. Slash the allowances toward the lip as necessary to release tension in the fabric, and fit the allowance around the scroll. Don't slash beyond the outside edge of the lip.

On the outside horizontal corner of the lip, fold a mitered corner downward, tucking the excess fabric between the frame and the cover (see page 64). Use dressmaker's pins to fit the miter. ▽

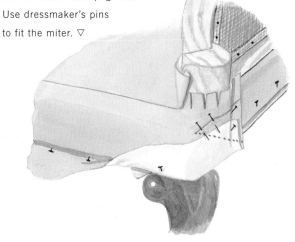

Slipstitch the miter fold closed, working from the front corner to the arm post. Hide thread knots inside the miter layers.

TIPS FROM THE PROS

✂Sometimes the miters don't follow the edge of the lip but sit on top of the lip, pointing diagonally from the corner toward the center of the deck. Duplicate the type of miter used on your old cover, but custom-fit it on the furniture.

✂If you stitch the miter by machine, keep the fitting pins in place but remove all the slip-tacks. Carefully remove the cover from the deck. Chalk-mark the inside of the miter fold, then repin the miter with the wrong side out and machine-stitch. Trim away the excess on the miter and deck as shown, leaving a $1/2$" seam allowance. ▽

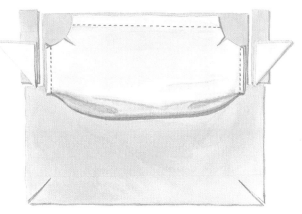

putting the cover on the deck or seat

At the back posts and the inside of the arm posts, turn under the slashed edges. Stretch and slip-tack them to the outside faces of the rails, just inside the posts. Slip-tack the deck cover side and back edges to the outside face of their rails. Slash the bottom lip allowance over the fullest part of the front leg to release tension. Stretch and slip-tack the lip side allowance onto the arm post (photo 17, page 118). ▽

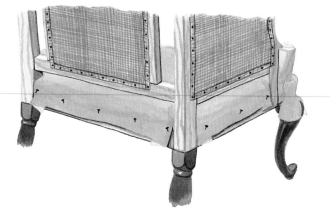

TIPS FROM THE PROS

✂ If you're reupholstering a complicated scroll arm like the one shown here, you may not know at this point how the fabric can best be finished along the back of the vertical scroll post. If you like you can wait, as we did, to slip-tack the lip ends until after the inside arm is installed, when you'll be better able to judge the best arrangement of the layers. Proceed now to the inside arm and return to this section later.

At the front of the arm post, manipulate the flanges of the slashed lip allowance down and inside between the padding and the post. Stretch and fit the bottom lip allowance down over both sides of the vertical corner. Tack it inside the ditch above the leg. Restretch the side lip allowance back over the outside face of the arm post. Clip as necessary to fit the curve of the post; stretch and tack it in place. ▷

TIPS FROM THE PROS

✂ Later you may be able to tack the lip flanges against a nearby frame member. To prepare for this, measure the drop of the lip. Thread a long, straight needle with twine and sew through each flange, about $1/2"-1"$ above the end; form a loop equal in length to the measurement taken. Knot the twine ends together. Push the twine loop through the lip/post crevice and pull the loop straight down and out through the webbing below. Later, after you thread the inside arm flanges down in the same way, stretch pairs of loops down and tack the flanges to the bottom of the scroll or nearest wood member. Use a staple gun for tacking up from the bottom through the spaces in the webbing to ensure that the flanges won't eventually work their way to the outside of the furniture.

Trim the excess fabric above the leg, following the bottom edge of the ditch. Trim the permanently tacked allowances about $1/2"$ outside the tacks. ▷

Stretch and permanently tack the front lip allowance to the bottom face of the rails on both sides of the front legs. Clip the allowance if necessary to fit it around rail contours so the cover fits taut against the frame. Trim away any excess allowances. ▽

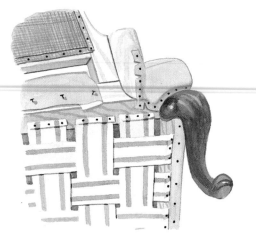

This club chair seat is very different from that of the wing chair. It advances straight forward from the back and drops down the front to join a welted boxing strip. Both pieces end at the front face of the arm post. ▽

Position the seat cover over its innards and padding. Slip-tack the back allowance to the bottom face of the back rail. Slip-tack the front allowance to the front face of the front rail. Make diagonal corner slashes for the back posts first, then turn the side allowances of the seat cover wrong side up, so that a fold is created along each inside arm from the front to the back. Make a straight slash aimed toward the back face of the arm post. ▽

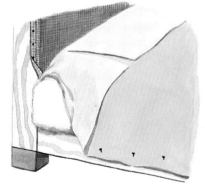

Push the cover side allowances to the outside between the arm liner and side rails. Work the corners of the cover out around each side of the back posts and arm posts. ▽

Slip-tack the seat cover to the outside face of the side and back rail. Check the cover for tightness over the frame. If necessary, remove the slip-tacks, restretch, then slip-tack again. On the sides and back, tack the cover securely, turning the slash edges under next to the posts. ▽

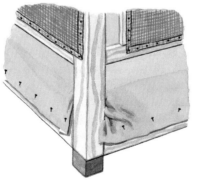

Check for smoothness at the front corners of the seat. Make a straight slash through the side allowance toward the corner of the top face of the front rail where it intersects the front face of the arm post. Stretch and tighten the front allowance down on the front face of the front rail, if necessary, and rearrange the slip-tacking. ▽

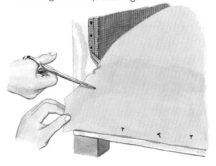

Stretch the front ends of the cover down again so that the slash rests at the intersection of the rail and post. Fill any corner hollows or dimples with extra padding by pushing it inside from the bottom with your regulator. Permanently tack the front allowance to the front face of the front rail. Permanently tack the ends to the front face of the arm post. Trim away any excess allowances. ▽

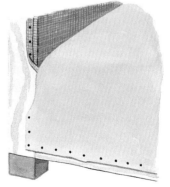

putting the cover on the inside arm, fascia, and wing

THE INSIDE ARM, FASCIA, AND WING

The inside arm of this wing chair has a double scroll with a fascia. The welting around the fascia continues down the back of the vertical scroll post to the bottom of the side rail. The fascia can be machine-sewn to the inside arm before it's installed on the chair, as explained below, or it can be applied afterward, as shown in photos 19–22, pages 118–19. If you'll be applying the fascia separately, refer as well to Other Inside Arm and Fascia Designs, pages 91–93. Every scroll arm chair is different, so refer to your stripping notes if you have any doubts about how to put together your new upholstery.

Placing the Padding

If you're replacing the stuffing, position it over the inside arm. Cover new or existing stuffing with a layer of padding, slashing it to fit. Permanently tack the top of the padding under the horizontal arm scroll and to the fascia; tuck it into the crevices between the inside arm and back and the inside arm and deck (photo 12, page 117). Trim away any excess padding.

Fitting a Machine-Sewn Fascia

Cut out the fascia and inside arm cover pieces, using the old cover as a cutting pattern. Working as follows, fit the fascia and inside arm covers on the furniture to make sure the fabric will fit smoothly around the scroll curves.

✄You can use the following method to check the fit of any shape fascia, as well as that of a flat-top scroll arm.

✄If your chair has an applied fascia, there's no need to check the fit now. You can proceed instead to Sewing the Fascia, opposite. Refer also to photos 13–21, pages 117–19.

Baste the fascia cover to the inside arm cover with the wrong sides of the fabric together. Baste on the stitching line, starting and stopping at the marked dots; clip the inside arm seam allowance as needed, making the clips as shallow and as few in number as possible. (The illustration shows the right inside arm and fascia.) ▷

Place the inside arm and fascia cover right side out over the padded frame. To temporarily secure the allowances on one side of the fascia, slip-tack the cover to the bottom and back of the scrolls for several inches, then smooth and stretch the cover to check the fit.

TIPS FROM THE PROS

✄An applied fascia can be soft with only padding under it, and slipstitched in place (photo 21, page 119), or it can be upholstered separately around a rigid plywood or cardboard form before it's attached.

✄To temporarily hold the inside arm cover to the padding, pin-tack it with dressmaker's pins. Use these pins also for fitting the seamlines.

✄Don't forget to fit pairs of cover pieces—those that appear at both ends of the furniture, such as a fascia—at the same time. Stand back and look at both covers to make sure they appear identical in size and shape.

If the fascia cover appears smooth and the seamlines align with the fascia frame perimeter, proceed with the sewing, opposite. However, if it appears to be too tight, loose, small, or large, then you can try one or more of the following to adjust it:

✄If the seamline follows the frame but the cover is puffy or loose, add more padding under the fascia.

✄If the seamline follows the frame but there's too much tension from the padding, or the outside allowance isn't smooth over the outside face, remove some padding from under the fascia.

✄If any part of the seamline is inside or outside the frame perimeter, cut the basting thread in that area and release a few stitches. Fit a new seamline, repinning the layers with the pins aligned with the frame perimeter. Use a curved needle and thread to baste the new seamline while the cover pieces are on the chair.

After fitting, remove the cover pieces from the chair. Chalk-mark any new seamlines on the wrong side of both pieces; make new cross-marks. Remove all the basting threads.

Sewing the Fascia

If you've not already done so, make all the welting you'll need for the entire chair. Refer to Sewing in Basic Construction Techniques (pages 72–74).

Cut a piece of welting long enough to fit the fascia perimeter and to continue to the bottom face of the side rail, plus another 10" for allowance. Remove 1" of the stitches and cut 1" of cord from one end of the welting.

Pin and machine-baste the welting to the seam allowance on the right side of the fascia (photo 20, page 119): Start with the trimmed cord end at the dot that marks the back of the vertical scroll, and stitch to the dot marking the bottom corner of the horizontal scroll. Make sure the welting stitching line is directly over the cover piece seamline. Clip the welting seam allowance as necessary.

✄ If your chair has an applied fascia, proceed to Attaching the Inside Arm, *right*.

TIPS FROM THE PROS

✄ Because you must sew with the welting on top and the seam allowance to the right of the needle, you'll have to sew one of the fascias from the bottom of the horizontal scroll to the top of the vertical scroll. To do this easily, allow a generous length of welting to go around the fascia and cut the cord from inside the end after sewing.

Sew the fascia cover to the inside arm cover with right sides together; start and stop at the same dots as for the welting, backstitching at each end. To release the fascia tacking allowance between the scrolls, clip the fascia seam allowance up to the dots. ▷

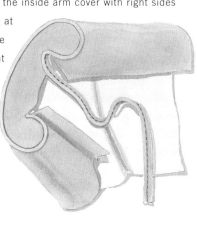

Attaching the Inside Arm

Position the inside arm/fascia cover over the arm front with the seam allowances facing away from the fascia. ▽

✄ If you're applying the fascia cover separately, pleat and slip-tack the front inside arm allowance to the fascia frame; refer to photo 18, page 118. Then continue to fit the inside arm as follows, omitting references to the fascia cover.

Smooth the inside arm cover toward the back. Fold the back of the cover forward in front of the wing. Slip-tack the top allowance under the horizontal scroll. Slip-tack the fascia outside allowance to the outside face of the fascia frame, clipping as necessary so the allowance lies flat against the frame. ▽

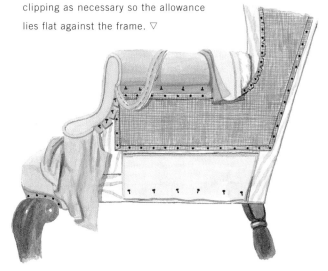

putting the cover on the inside arm, fascia, and wing

Smooth the inside arm cover flat around the vertical scroll post; smooth the fabric folded across the arm top. In front of the post, make slashes straight up from the bottom edge so the cover lies smoothly on top of the lip. Don't trim these flanges.

Smooth the cover over the arm and down toward the deck. Cut an angled slash from the bottom edge toward the back face of the vertical scroll; refer to photo 16, page 118. This cut is one of two that will enable you to pull the bottom allowance through to the outside. ▽

Smooth and stretch the inside arm cover from front to back along the roll of the horizontal scroll. Adjust the slip-tacking under the scroll, if necessary, so that the cover fits smoothly against the frame. Adjust the back of the inside arm so that the fold is against the front face of the wing. Slash a Y-cut in the folded-back layer; aim it toward the front face of the wing (photo 14, page 117). This slash divides the inside arm cover into inside and outside sections. ▷

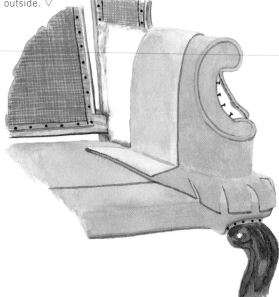

If necessary, adjust the slip-tacking holding the side allowance of the cover around the vertical scroll to a tighter fit. On the side drop in front of the vertical scroll, trim away all but 2" of excess fabric. ▷

Unfold the fabric and permanently tack the pointed flange from the Y-cut slash to the front face of the wing. Smooth and stretch the inside cover section backwards; slip-tack the slashed edge to the frame member underneath, ending at the inside face of the back post.

✂ If you're installing the cover over existing stuffing, you won't be able to tack the slash to the front or bottom of the inside wing. Just smooth the fabric toward the back and slip-tack it to the back post. The inside wing cover will secure the slashed edge later.

Fold the back allowance forward again and slash a Y-cut near the bottom of the back edge; aim it toward the front face of the back liner. Unfold the fabric and smooth the inside arm down and back, spreading the Y-cut around the back liner. Permanently tack the triangular flange from the cut to the front face of the back liner.

Smooth the inside arm below the liner down and back so that it fits flat against the intersection of the inside arm and deck. Then fold forward the back allowance below the Y-cut so it lies on the deck. Cut an angled slash in the fabric folded back on the deck; start at the bottom edge and aim toward the corner of the back post. This is the second slash that will enable you to pull the bottom allowance of the inside arm to the outside. ▽

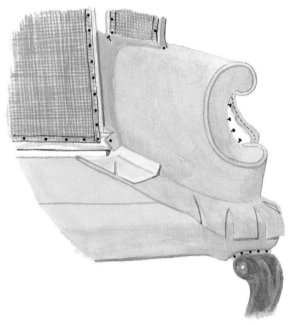

Push the bottom allowance to the outside through the crevice between the deck and inside arm (photo 13, page 117). Working from the outside of the side rail, pull and stretch the bottom allowance down; slip-tack it toward the front and back ends of the side rail. Fold under the slashed edges at the ends and slip-tack.

If necessary, adjust the length of the slashes around the front of the vertical scroll; work from the deck side of the chair and then tighten the slip-tacks at the back of the vertical scroll so the cover fits snugly.

Use your regulator to insert the flanges lying on top of the lip between the vertical scroll and the stuffing/padding on the lip. Leave the allowance hanging over the side drop.

TIPS FROM THE PROS

✂ These long flanges can be easily tacked to the hidden bottom area of the vertical scroll. Attach twine loops to each flange and permanently tack them to the frame as described in The Deck or Seat (page 80).

Remove the slip-tacks holding the fabric at the back of the vertical scroll. Fold under the vertical front edge of the scroll cover. Insert a cardboard tacking strip inside the fold and blind-tack the front edge to the outside face of the scroll. ▽

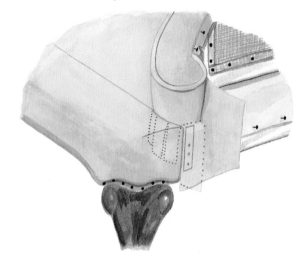

TIPS FROM THE PROS

✂ If you left the end of the lip allowance free, be sure to slip-tack it before tacking the front edge of the inside arm to the vertical scroll. Decide first if it would be better to finish this area by folding the lip edge over the front edge of the scroll.
✂ Here's an alternative to blind-tacking the front edge on the scroll: Simply fold the vertical front edge of the scroll cover under, stretch and pull the folded edge down and under to the bottom face of the side rail, and permanently tack it in place.

putting the cover on the inside arm, fascia, and wing

Stretch the vertical scroll cover section to the back of the scroll again; permanently tack it in place. Trim away the allowance beyond the tacks. Permanently tack the outside face of the fascia.

Permanently tack the top allowance of the outer section of the inside arm cover under the horizontal scroll and around the curve at its back (photo 15, page 117). Trim away the allowance beyond the tacks at the back, or stretch and permanently tack it to the outside face of the back post. Trim away any excess.

Slash the bottom allowance below the vertical scroll as necessary so it can be turned to the bottom face of the side rail. ▽

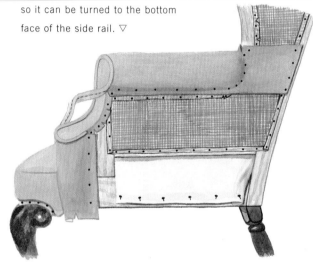

TIPS FROM THE PROS

✂ Don't forget to stand back and look at both arms together. Be sure any fabric pattern is aligned as you wish, and check that the shape appears balanced. Poke in loose stuffing if necessary.

Stretch down the bottom allowance below the outside of the vertical scroll; permanently tack it to the bottom face of the side rail.

Working from the back of the chair, stretch and pull the back allowance of the inside arm, and slip-tack it in place to the back face of the back post.

Permanently tack the top allowance from the arm Y-cut to the inside wing frame members. Turn under the long edges of the other Y-cut around the back liner, and slip-tack to the back face of the back post. ▽

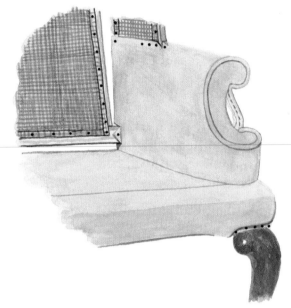

Stretch and pull the remainder of the back and bottom allowances to the back face of the back post under the back liner. Turn under the slashed edge; slip-tack it and the remainder of the piece in place. ▷

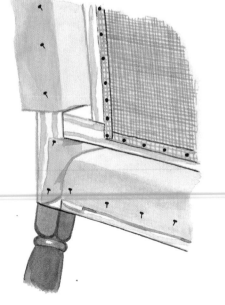

✂If you didn't sew the fascia to the inside arm before installing the inside arm, position the fascia on the furniture now. Pin-tack it through the welting seamline. Using a curved needle, blindstitch it to the inside arm; refer to page 68 and also to photo 21 on page 119.

Attaching the Inside Wing

Now that the inside arm is completed, you're ready to reupholster the inside wing. Position the inside wing cover over the unstuffed inside wing.

✂If you're installing the cover over existing stuffing and padding, check the position of the inside wing as described below, remove it, sew welting to the bottom allowance, install the inside wing, then slipstitch the lower edge over the top edge of the inside arm. Refer to photos 23–24, page 119.

✂If you're not installing the cover over the previous stuffing and padding, tack the horizontal welting on now with the seam allowance facing upward.

Turn under the bottom allowance, and insert a cardboard tacking strip inside the fold. Hold the tacking strip in position at the center of the fold and position the cover wrong side out against the bottom of the inside wing. Blind-tack the bottom edge. ◁

Place the stuffing/padding layers over the inside wing and the front and top faces of the wing. Align the bottom of the stuffing/padding with the bottom of the tacking strip. Lift the inside wing cover up and smooth through the center to the top of the wing frame; slip-tack the top allowance to the outside wing.

TIPS FROM THE PROS

✂You can position the stuffing/padding against the inside wing before blind-tacking the bottom allowance. If you do, fold up their bottom edges several inches above the bottom of the wing and hold them out of the way with upholsterer's pins while you blind-tack. Remove the pins and align the bottom edges of the stuffing/padding with the bottom of the cardboard tacking strip.

✂Depending upon the size and shape of your chair, you may find it easier to work on the bottom edge of the wing if you turn the chair onto its side. If you do, turn it upright again to work on the top edge.

Continue smoothing and stretching the cover up and out on each side of the top. Slip-tack the front allowance to the outside face of the wing and the back allowance to the outside face of the back post.

As you near the top corner on the back post, cut a horizontal slash at the bottom face of the top rail so that the back allowance separates. Slip-tack the top area to the front face of the top rail. ▽

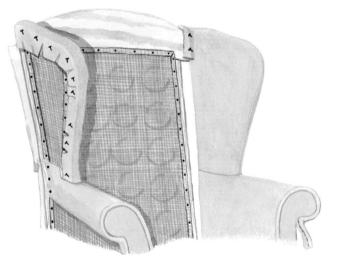

Working from the outside of the wing, clip the allowances and excess fabric as necessary so that the cover is smooth and taut around the top and front of the wing. There's no need to notch out the excess; any bulk will be covered later by the welting and flexible metal tacking strips of the outside wing. Slip-tack these curved areas on the outside of the wing.

✄ At the top outside corner, stretch and fold the top allowance into a miter; slip-tack.

✄ At the bottom of the wing, pull the folded-under allowance tightly to the outside wing and slip-tack.

Tacking on the Welting

Starting at the horizontal scroll, permanently tack the loose welting to the outside face of the fascia and behind the vertical scroll. Clean-finish the welting end even with the bottom edge of the side rail. ▷

TIPS FROM THE PROS

✄ Don't forget, you may need to slip-tack a cover section, remove the tacks, smooth, stretch, and slip-tack again several times before achieving the fit you desire. You won't know for sure that the inside arms and wings are perfect until you've installed the inside back.

Planning Ahead for the Cushion

If you plan to reuse your old inside cushion, check its fit against the inside arms to make sure the stuffing and contours appear identical on both arms. If they don't, remove some of the slip-tacks and poke in some additional stuffing. Bear in mind that when the new cover with its welting goes over the inner cushion, it will fit more snugly.

Finishing the Inside Arm and Inside Wing

Later, after you've installed the inside back and you're satisfied with the fit of all the inside sections, permanently tack all the slip-tacked areas on the top and front faces of the wing, and then trim away any excess fabric beyond the tacks.

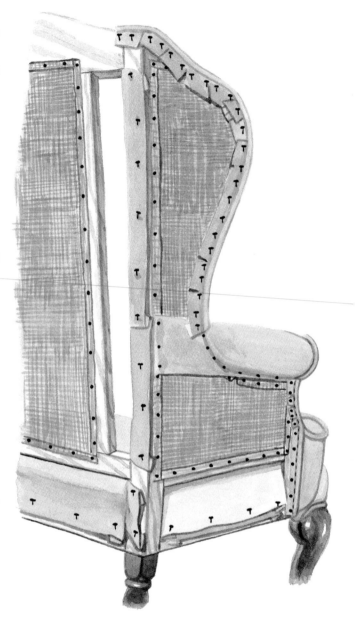

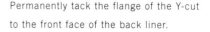

Many pieces of furniture feature single-scroll arms with an applied rigid fascia; these are treated a little differently than our more ornate double-scroll wing chair. On the following example the horizontal scroll continues on the outside to the back post, the tight seat is straight rather than a T shape, and the fascia cover is applied to the arm front after the inside and outside arms are installed.

✂ If you're reupholstering a piece with a soft fascia that you'll blindstitch in place, read this section, pleat the inside arm fabric onto the fascia frame as appropriate, and refer to photos 19–21 on pages 118–19.

✂ If your furniture has decorative pleats on the front of the arm, refer to this section to install the inside arm, but turn to pages 62–63 to see how to arrange and secure the pleats. ▽

Installing the Inside Arm

Position and smooth the inside arm cover over the stuffing and padding; tuck the bottom allowance into the inside arm/seat crevice to hold the fabric in place.

Working from the outside of the arm, slip-tack the top allowance under the scroll of the arm from front to back. Leave the area at the back edge free so you'll be able to fit the back of the inside arm cover around the back post.

Smooth the front allowance around the front face of the inside arm and slip-tack it in the vertical area first. Then, form and slip-tack fan-shape pleats around the curved front face of the scroll to tidy the extra fabric. You can turn fan-shaped pleats in either direction; they'll be hidden by the fascia. ▽

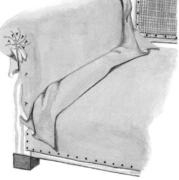

Smooth the inside arm cover straight back to the back post. Pull out enough of the tucked-in bottom allowance at the back so you can fold the back allowance forward onto the arm. Starting at the edge of the back allowance, slash a Y-cut to enable the cover to fit around the back liner. Then, cut an angled slash from the top edge of the Y-cut to the front outside corner of the back post. ▽

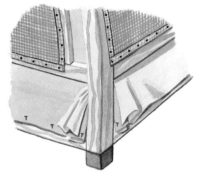

Permanently tack the flange of the Y-cut to the front face of the back liner.

Cut a diagonal slash through the bottom allowance to the inside corner of the back post as explained for the wing chair (refer to page 87). Pull the bottom allowance outside between the arm liner and side rail. Pull the back allowance outside between the back liner and back rail. ▽

Slip-tack the bottom allowance to the outside face of the side rail, stopping several inches from the arm post.

Stretch and slip-tack the back allowance of the outside portion of the cover to the back face of the back post. Slip-tack the back allowance of the inside portion over it. ▽

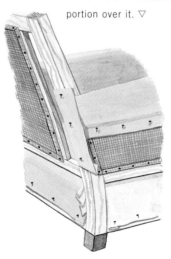

an inside arm with a rigid fascia

From the outside of the furniture, just behind the arm post, pull the bottom allowance of the cover down over the side rail until it's taut; on the wrong side of the fabric, chalk-mark the intersection of the inside face of the arm post and the top face of the side rail.

Pull the bottom allowance out to the front of the chair. To establish an allowance for tacking the front edge of the inside arm to the front of the arm post, judge the allowance width needed at the bottom edge of the post and slash from this point diagonally toward the chalk-marked corner. Remove slip-tacking as necessary along the side rails while you do this. ▽

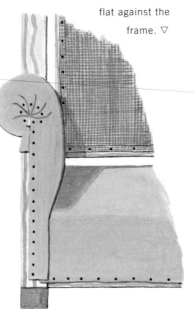

On the side pull the bottom allowance through to the outside again. Smooth, stretch, and slip-tack the bottom allowance to the outside face of the side rail.

At the front face of the arm post, pull and stretch the front part of the angled slash forward and down. Insert more padding under this area, if necessary, to fill out the inside arm between the arm post and the seat. Permanently tack the front allowance, including the pleated area, to the arm post; trim away any excess fabric and tack so that all fabric folds and edges are flat against the frame. ▽

Installing the Rigid Fascia

On a chair or sofa of this shape, you install the inside back and the outside arm before installing the applied fascia. These are explained later in this chapter. You can prepare the fascia as explained below now or wait until you're ready to apply it.

✂ If your furniture has front boxing under the seat between the arm posts, install it before you install the fascia.

Cut a piece of padding the same shape as the fascia frame, adding enough extra all around to cover the thickness of the frame. Center the padding on the wrong side of the fascia cover. Top it with the frame. ▽

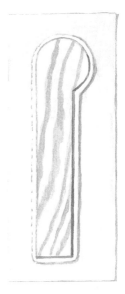

Fold the bottom cover allowance onto the wrong side of the frame; glue it in place. Add a dot of glue to the center top of the frame; fold the allowance to the wrong side. Fold the long, straight edge of the fascia cover to the wrong side and glue it in place near the edge; stop where the frame begins to curve.

Trim the long, straight side allowance to 1". On the opposite side allowance, make a diagonal slash toward the bottom corner of the scroll. ▽

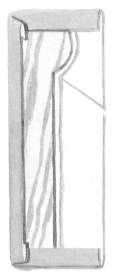

Glue the side allowance in place from the bottom to the slash. Trim the excess to 1". Around the scroll trim the allowances to one-half the scroll diameter. Form shallow pleats that overlap as little as possible; glue them in place. ▷

TIPS FROM THE PROS

✂You can slip-tack the pleats to hold them in place for gluing.

✂You can slip-tack and then permanently tack all the allowances onto the fascia frame instead of gluing them. Follow the same working order as for gluing.

Cut a piece of welting to fit around all but the bottom edge of the fascia, plus enough to turn under at both ends. Finish the ends. Glue the welting to the wrong side of the fascia so that the cord extends beyond the frame. Clip and notch the welting flange as necessary. ▷

Position the covered fascia right side up over the front face of the arm post; align the bottom edge with the bottom of the arm post. To mark the fascia position, push dressmaker's pins straight into the inside arm fabric, outside the fascia welting. Remove the fascia, and add glue to the welting seam allowance. Reposition the fascia on the arm post. Add several slip-tacks between the fascia and welting to secure it while the glue cures.

TIPS FROM THE PROS

✂You can attach the fascia with finishing nails. Space the nails about 6" apart along the center of the fascia and drive them through it, into the arm post. Use your mallet when the nails near the fabric. If the nails do not disappear under the fabric, insert a dressmaker's pin through the fabric and gently lift it up and over each nail. Close the hole by rubbing gently with your fingernail. ▽

putting the cover on the inside back

THE INSIDE BACK

The inside back is the last piece to be installed on the inside of the furniture and it's the last for which you'll have to make tricky fitting cuts. Once the inside back is in place, you should stand back and check the look of all the inside upholstery to be sure it's balanced, and then you can permanently tack all the allowances that have only been slip-tacked.

Placing the Padding

If you're replacing the stuffing, position it on the inside back. Cover new or existing stuffing with a new layer of padding. Push the bottom allowance of the padding to the outside through the crevice between the deck and the inside back. Permanently tack the top allowance to the back face of the top rail. Fold the side allowances onto the inside back, slash them above the bottom liner and below the top rail, then push the allowance between the slashes through the side crevice. Trim the excess padding at the slashed areas, leaving enough to tuck into the crevices.

Attaching the Fabric

Position the inside back cover. Push the bottom allowance to the outside through the crevice between the deck and the inside back; slip-tack it to the center area of the back face on the back rail. Smooth and stretch the cover straight upward. Slip-tack the top allowance to the center of the back face of the top rail (photo 25, page 120). ▽

On the inside of the chair, turn back the cover side allowance to form a fold against the inside arm and wing.

Poke your fingers between the inside arm and back to find the back liner. Slash a Y-cut through the side allowance; aim it toward the end of the liner.

At the bottom of the top rail, cut a straight slash through the side allowance; aim it toward the inside corner of the back post and inside wing (photo 26, page 120). ▽

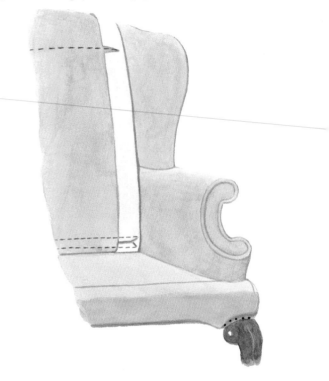

Between the two slashes push the side allowance through the back/wing crevice to the outside. Smooth and stretch the inside back horizontally across the center toward the sides. Working from the back, slip-tack the side allowances to the inside face of the back post directly over the tacked allowance from the inside wing. Continuing to smooth and stretch the cover out and up, and out and down, slip-tack the side allowance between the top rail and back liner. At the Y-cut fold the flange to the wrong side over the front face of the liner.

Finish slip-tacking the bottom allowance; at the back posts fold the side allowance edges back over themselves for reinforcement.

Slip-tack the top allowance toward the inside corners. On each side, above the slash for the top rail, turn under the allowance so that the vertical fold is against the inside wing (photo 27 page 120). Pull and stretch the fold upward and onto the back face of the top rail, and slip-tack.

Examine the inside back and other sections from the front of the chair. If adjustments are necessary, remove the slip-tacks, adjust the cover, and then slip-tack again. ▽

If you plan to reuse the loose deck cushion, check its fit again now. If you plan to make a new inner cushion, you can make the cutting pattern now, if you wish (refer to The Loose Cushion, pages 104–108). You can make the cushion cover at any time now that the inside upholstery is complete.

When no further adjustments are necessary, permanently tack all the deck or seat, inside arm, inside wing, and inside back allowances. When finished, trim away the excess fabric beyond the tacks (photo 28, page 120). Trim the padding even with the back post. ▽

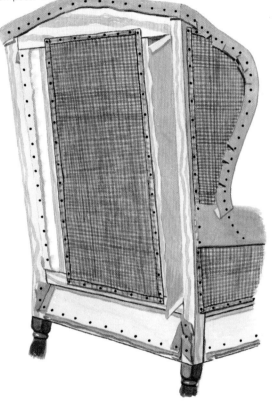

TIPS FROM THE PROS

If you trim the vertical allowances about 1" outside the back post, they'll be long enough to tuck into the space between the post and back slat. This will keep them out of the way of the outside back cover. If you trim them closer to the post than 1", they'll be too short to stay put and are likely to poke out against the outside back padding.

other inside back designs

Three alternative inside back configurations are discussed here.

COVERING AN ARMLESS BACK

If you're covering an armless chair or sofa, your task is simple in comparison to redoing an armchair. You'll need to make fewer fitting cuts, because the side allowances need not be slashed to fit around the back or arm rails; they're simply stretched around the frame and tacked to the back face of the back posts. Refer to your old cover and stripping notes to see how to install the new inside back.

✄If your furniture has a scroll shoulder, duplicate the construction of the original upholstery. You can probably handle it as you would the front of a scroll arm.

✄If your furniture has side boxing, duplicate the construction of the original upholstery. ▽

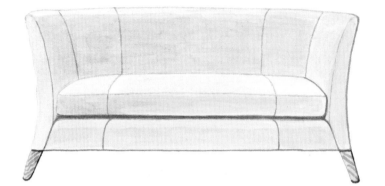

COVERING A WIDE TIGHT BACK

If you're reupholstering a wide sofa for which the inside back must be pieced, such as the one above, sew the sections together before installing the cover, then apply them as one piece. Refer to Measuring and Estimating, and to your chart and notes, to plan and cut the pieces. △

Machine-stitch the side panels to the center panel with $1/2$" seams. Edgestitch the seams to hold them open. ▽

Install the inside back cover on this sofa in the same manner as for the wing chair. They both have a tight back covered with a rectangular fabric piece that you shape directly on the frame.

COVERING A SPLIT-BACK

An inside back configured like the one shown below is called a *split-back* because the seams between the panels are tacked to the frame, creating a puffed effect. The stuffing and padding are installed individually on each section. ▽

✄There are a number of different techniques for installing the inside back cover on a split-back, some quite different from the method described here. Duplicate the method and seam allowance width of your old cover.

Sewing Panels for a Split-Back Inside Back

Refer to Measuring and Estimating and to your chart and notes to plan the size of each panel, measuring for the width of the center panel between the indentations and for the side panels from the indentation to the point where they meet the outside back. Add a $1/2$" seam allowance to the indentation edges; to all other edges add the standard allowances.

Cut a 9"-wide muslin pull-through piece the same length as the indentation seam.

Place the side panel over the center panel with the right sides together and the indentation edges aligned. Place the muslin pull-through over the side panel. Sew through all three layers. ▽

Installing the Center Panel on a Split-Back

Position the center cover panel over the stuffing and padding on the center of the inside back. Slip-tack the center of the top allowance to the back face of the top rail.

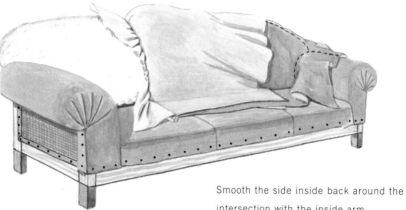

Pull and stretch out the center panel horizontally across the center, and push the muslin pull-through between the stuffing and padding crevice to the outside of the furniture. △

Make sure the muslin pull-through goes around the outside face of the back slat. Pull through the inside back bottom allowances. Slip-tack the center of the bottom allowance to the back face of the back rail. Continue slip-tacking the top and bottom as far as possible toward the back slats. Duplicate any slashes on the old cover and finish slip-tacking the top and bottom. Stretch and slip-tack the muslin pull-through to the back face of the back slats.

Check the center panel from the front of the sofa. If it's smooth and balanced, proceed to the side panels.

Installing the Side Panels on a Split-Back

Smooth and slip-tack the bottom and and then the top allowances of the side panels. Duplicate the bottom corner slash from the old cover, and release enough bottom slip-tacks so the bottom allowance will be on the seat, allowing you to fit the side allowance around the inside arm.

Smooth the side inside back around the intersection with the inside arm. Smoothing the fabric onto the arm and down toward the seat, make any necessary fitting slashes; start at the outside edge. ▽

Use your regulator to manipulate these long flanges through the crevice between the arm and inside back. Stretch them out and down, then permanently tack them over the flanges from the inside arm onto the back face of the curved arm rail.

Permanently tack all allowances and trim away the excess.

putting the cover on the outside arm and wing

THE OUTSIDE ARM AND WING

This wing chair has a one-piece outside wing/outside arm. Some other outside arm configurations are discussed later in this section.

✂ If you've not yet installed the burlap on the outside wing/outside arm, you can wait to do so until the welting and flexible tacking strips have been attached; refer to photo 32, page 121.

✂ If your furniture has a front boxing strip, install it now, before upholstering the outside arm and wing. Refer to The Border and Skirt, pages 109–11.

Attaching the Welting

Cut a piece of welting long enough to go from fascia to fascia under the arms, around the wings, and along the top of the back; allow some extra. Finish one end. With the cord facing up and the flange facing down, position the finished end against the fascia under one of the horizontal arm scrolls. Slip-tack the end. With one hand guide the welting under the arm, up around the wing, across the back, and down the other side, slip-tacking the flange to the frame with the other hand (photo 29, page 121). Check that the welting follows the curves smoothly, then finish the other end next to the other fascia and permanently tack the welting to the frame.

Attaching the Tacking Strip

The easiest and quickest way to finish the wing top and front edges is with a flexible tacking strip. Tack a flexible tacking strip along the front edge of the outside wing, under the horizontal scroll, along the fascia and along the back of the vertical post (refer to Securing Fabric to the Frame, pages 57–61, and photo 30, page 121). ▷

Leaving a $1/8$" gap, press the jaws of the flexible tacking strip nearly closed with your fingers (photo 31, page 121).

TIPS FROM THE PROS

✂ The flexible tacking strip can be installed in one continuous piece from one wing across the top of the back and then along the second wing, but you may find such a long piece awkward to handle. There's no reason you can't cut the strip and apply it in shorter pieces.

✂ If the flexible tacking strip must turn a sharp outside corner, as it does between the fascia and horizontal scroll on our chair, cut and piece it so there's a gripping portion of the jaw on each side of the corner—if you position a space between grippers at the bend, there won't be anything to secure the corner of the cover fabric.

✂ Instead of using flexible tacking strips, you can finish the front edges of the outside arm/wing piece with a blindstitch. Attach the padding and position the cover as follows. Then, when you've completed permanently tacking the bottom and back allowances of the outside arm/wing cover, trim the remaining cut edges $1/2$" beyond the welting stitches. Turn under the trimmed edges to the wrong side, align the fold against the welting seam, and pin-tack with dressmaker's pins, clipping as necessary for curves. Using a curved needle blindstitch the fold to the welting seam.

Attaching the Padding

If you wish, place the chair on its side. Position a sheet of padding over the outside arm and wing; permanently tack it to the outside face of the posts and rails; on the edges with tacking strips, tack inside the inner folded edge of the tacking strip. Following the jaw edge of the tacking strip and the frame of the chair, trim away the excess batting (photo 33, page 122). ▽

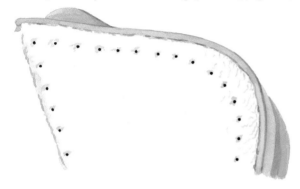

If the chair is on its side, turn it upright. Using the regulator, tuck the front and top cover edge into the jaw of the flexible tacking strip. ▽

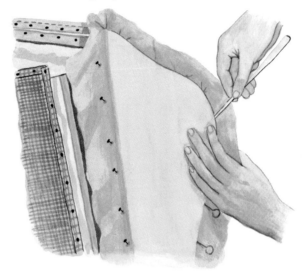

Attaching the Fabric

Position the cover over the outside arm and wing, aligning any motifs appropriately. Slip-tack the cover to the bottom face of the side rail, tacking as close to the back leg as possible, then wrap the side allowance onto the back face of the back post and slip-tack above the leg. Smooth and stretch the fabric up to the top of the wing; pin-tack between the jaws of the tacking strip and the welting. Pin-tack the entire front edge (photo 34, page 122). Stretch and slip-tack the back allowances to the back face of the back post. ▷

Check the cover for smoothness. Adjust, if necessary, by pulling out the allowance and then pushing it back into the flexible tacking strip. Trim the cover edge and close the jaw (refer to pages 60–61 and photos 35–37, pages 122–23).

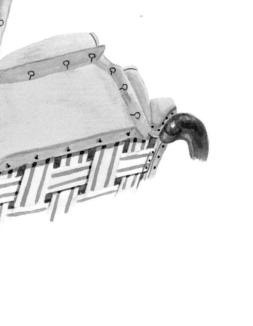

putting the cover on the outside arm and wing

On the lower edge of the chair, slash the bottom allowance up to the frame at the front face of the back leg. Trim the allowance over the leg, behind the slash, to 2"; turn it under so that the fold is even with the bottom edge of the rail (photo 38, page 123). Slip-tack the allowance to the back face of the back post. Permanently tack the bottom allowance to the bottom face of the side rail. ▽

Tighten the fabric if necessary by stretching it more around the back post. Permanently tack the back allowance to the back face of the back post. Repeat the process on the other side of the chair. ▽

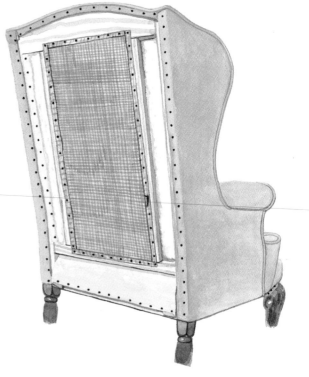

other outside arm designs

A wing with a flat-top arm may look quite different from the chair with the double-scroll fascia, but you can apply its one-piece outside arm/wing cover in the same manner. For a two-piece outside arm/wing cover, attach the outside wing cover along its bottom edge first; next attach the top and front curves; and then secure the back allowance. Add the rectangular outside arm piece beneath the wing as follows.

Most outside arm covers are rectangular. The tacking order for rectangular covers is the opposite of that for the wing chair. Blind-tack the top edge of the cover first; the cardboard tacking strip provides a sharp top edge. ▽

Install a flexible tacking strip on the front edge, if you wish. Alternatively, plan to use a rigid metal tacking strip to finish the front edge; refer to Securing Fabric to the Frame, pages 57–61 and photos 39 and 40, page 123.

Permanently tack the padding in place, then trim it. Fold down the cover over the padding; slip-tack the bottom edge first, then slip-tack the back edge while simultaneously pin-tacking the front edge to the welting seamline.

THE OUTSIDE BACK

The method for installing the outside back is the same for almost any style of furniture. If the top edge of your piece is curved, you may have to slash the top allowance in order to fit it into the flexible tacking strip.

✂If you've not yet installed burlap on the outside back, you can wait to do so until the welting and flexible tacking strip have been attached.

Attaching the Welting

Cut a piece of welting the length of the back post, plus some extra. Finish one end. With the cord extending beyond the frame and the flange on the back face, place the finished end at the bottom of one back post; tack permanently. Guide the welting up the post with one hand and tack it in place with the other. At the top, trim and finish the end of the welting and tack it. Repeat on the other back post.

Attaching the Tacking Strip

Install flexible tacking strips along the back posts and top rail. Starting at the bottom on one back post, permanently tack the strip up the post, across the top, and down the other post; use three pieces if you prefer. ▽

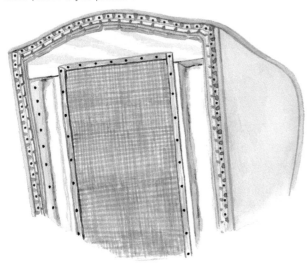

Leaving a 1/8" gap, press the jaws of the flexible tacking strip nearly closed with your fingers.

TIPS FROM THE PROS

✂If you prefer, you can use a rigid metal tacking strip instead of a flexible strip along the sides of the back cover. Apply the flexible strip to the top edge only, position and secure the cover on the top and bottom edges, and then secure the sides. (You might think the fabric would then be too tight for this to work, but it does work.) Refer to Securing Fabric to the Frame, pages 57–61, and photos 39 and 40, page 123. Piece the rigid tacking strips, if necessary.

Attaching the Padding

If you wish, lean the chair forward against the horses. Place the padding over the outside back and permanently tack it inside the flexible tacking strip edges and to the bottom rail. Trim the padding even with the jaw of the flexible tacking strip and the bottom face of the back rail.

Attaching the Fabric

Position the cover over the outside back of the furniture, aligning any motifs appropriately. Slip-tack the bottom allowance to the bottom face of the back rail.

Smooth and stretch the fabric straight up. Pin-tack the top allowance between the jaw of the tacking strip and the welting. Smooth the sides up and out toward the top; work from the center out and pin-tack the entire top allowance.

Starting at the center of the outside back, smooth the cover out horizontally and pin-tack the center of the sides. Pin-tack the top half of the side allowances by smoothing and stretching the fabric out and up. On the bottom half, smooth the fabric out and down.

On the lower edge of the chair, slash the bottom allowance up to the frame at the inside face of each back leg. Trim the allowance over the leg, outside the slash, to 2"; turn it under so the fold is even with the bottom edge of the rail. Stretch the allowance around the back post; pin-tack it between the jaw of the tacking strip and the welting.

Check the smoothness of the entire outside back cover. Make sure there are no wrinkles in the fabric along any of the edges.

Using the regulator, push the top allowance of the cover into the jaw of the flexible tacking strip. ▽

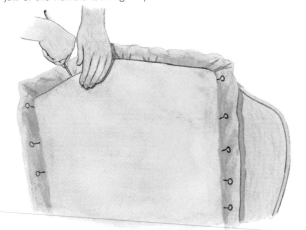

Check the outside back cover for smoothness again. Adjust, if necessary, by pulling out the allowance and then pushing it back into the tacking strip. Trim the allowance beyond the jaw of the tacking strip and close the jaw; start at the center and work out, stopping about 1" from each corner.

Insert the side allowances into the jaw of the flexible tacking strip. Check the fit and trim the excess fabric. ▽

Close the jaw, starting at the center and working down and then up. At the bottom make sure the folded allowance is securely enclosed. At each top corner manipulate the allowance smoothly around from side to top and close the jaw completely.

FINISHING

Your reupholstery is nearly complete. All that remains to be done is to add the welting to the lower edge and install the dust cover.

Adding Welting to the Bottom Rail

Cut a piece of welting long enough to rim the bottom of the chair, plus some extra. Positioning it so the cord extends beyond the frame, permanently tack the welting along the bottom face of the back rail: Start at the center and leave about 2" free before placing the first tack; tack up to the first back leg. Place a line of glue into the groove between the exposed leg and the rail, then insert the seam allowance of the welting into this groove. In this manner, tack and glue the remainder of the welting. Lap the ends, trim the cord, and fold the bias covering over the join (refer to page 74). ▽

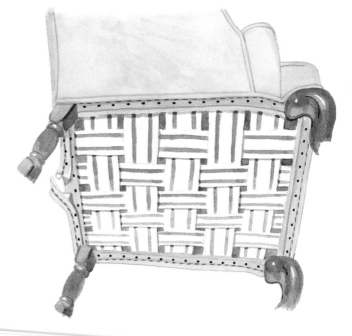

TIPS FROM THE PROS

✄ If there are no grooves above the legs on your furniture, at each leg trim the welting flange close to the stitching and glue it in place. Refer to photo 41, page 124.

Installing the Dust Cover

Turn the chair over. Measure the length and width of the bottom across the center; add 2" to each measurement and cut a piece of cambric this size.

Turn under about 1" on the front and back edges of the cambric, and permanently tack them to the center bottom face of the front and back rails. Turn under the same amount at the sides, and permanently tack them to the center bottom face of the side rails.

✂ If your bottom rails have single welting, fold under the edges so they align with the welting stitching line.

✂ If your bottom rails have no welting, position the folded edges of the dust cover about $1/2$" inside the outer edge of the rails.

Working from the centers out, fold and tack the front and back edges of the dust cover to the bottom of the rails; stop a short distance from the legs. Tack the sides in the same manner.

At each leg, diagonally fold back the corner of the dust cover; make a diagonal corner slash. ▽

Trim the points from the ends of the slashed edges, leaving about 1". ▽

Turn under each slash edge so that the fold aligns with the side of the leg; trim the excess fabric if necessary. Permanently tack the folded edges in place (photo 42, page 124). ▽

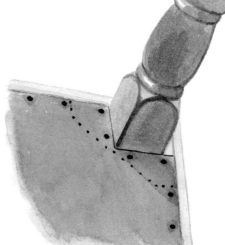

TIPS FROM THE PROS

✂ If you're redoing a fairly new chair, it's quite likely that the springs are stapled to the deck webbing. The ends of these staples are dangerously sharp. Place a layer of padding between the webbing and the dust cover, being careful not to run your fingers over the staples as you work.

putting the cover on the loose cushion

THE LOOSE CUSHION

A loose cushion has two parts: the inner cushion and the cover, which matches the upholstery. The inner cushion can be foam covered with polyester padding or ticking filled with loose polyester stuffing. The cushion cover should be secured with a slot zipper centered on the back boxing strip, which should be long enough to wrap around the back corners and extend onto the sides for 3". The back boxing must be cut in two pieces so it can accommodate the zipper; the front boxing is cut in one piece.

Make loose back cushions the same way you do seat cushions. Refer to the following directions, but make a cutting pattern over the inside back of the furniture and insert the zipper into the bottom boxing strip.

TIPS FROM THE PROS

✂ If the old inner cushion is comfortable and structurally sound, you can reuse it without taking it apart. After you insert it into the new cover, poke one or two layers of polyester batting between each broad side of the inner cushion and cover. This extra padding will make up for any condensing of the stuffing that occurred during previous use.

✂ If you're really pleased with your reupholstery, why not treat yourself to a down-filled inner cushion? Ask a professional to have one made for you.

Making the Top/Bottom Cutting Pattern

To make a boxed cushion that fits your furniture perfectly, first make a cutting pattern of the deck shape from muslin or a similar fabric. If your old cushion fits the reupholstered furniture, you can take its cover apart and use the pieces as cutting patterns.

To make the top/bottom cover cutting pattern, first cut a piece of muslin 3" larger than the greatest length and width of the deck. Position the muslin on the deck so that the allowance is equal all around. Smooth the muslin over the deck and against the inside back and arms; arrange the back corners first by running your fingers along the deck/back intersection, then arrange the sides.

Clip down into the side allowances so the muslin curves around the front of the inside arm; if you're making a T-shape cushion, trim all but a few inches of the excess fabric along the inside arms. Use dressmaker's pins to pin-tack as necessary.

Chalk-mark the back, inside arms, and outside and front edges on the lip. Be sure to hold the chalk upright so it won't disappear into the crevices. It's quite likely that the back edge will be somewhat curved to fit the contour of the inside back. Refer to photo 43, page 124. ▽

Remove the muslin cutting pattern from the furniture and fold it in half, chalk side out, matching the front and back corners. Pin the layers together on the chalk lines on one half. Turn the muslin over to see if the marks align; if they don't, split the difference and draw a new chalk outline.

TIPS FROM THE PROS

✂ If there's a big difference between the lines on the halves of the cutting pattern, the stuffing and padding may be not be balanced. However, it's just as likely that you didn't hold the chalk perfectly upright while marking, so try making another pattern before you decide to adjust the upholstery!

On each side edge make a dot 3" from the back corner to mark the seamline between the front and back boxing strips. Also mark the front and back centers. Add a ¹/₂" seam allowance all around, measuring from the outermost edge of the chalk line. ▷

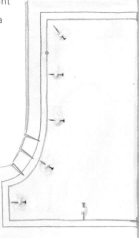

TIPS FROM THE PROS

✂ Use dressmaker's tracing paper and a tracing wheel to transfer the seam and cutting lines from one half of the pattern to the other.

Cushions for wide furniture: If you're making a cutting pattern for a sofa that has several separate cushions, make one wide cutting pattern as described above, then divide the pattern for the cushions by following the design details on the furniture, such as the seams on the back, by marking them on the muslin at the inside back and on the front lip. Remove the cutting pattern from the sofa and draw straight lines to connect the marks. Mark dots on the back of these lines for the boxing seams. Slash the large cutting pattern apart along the lines to form separate cushion patterns. Use only one of the end patterns to make both end cushion covers. When cutting out the covers, be sure to add a ¹/₂" seam allowance on the cut-apart edges. ▽

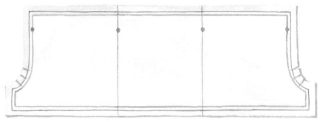

Making the Boxing Strip Cutting Patterns

To determine the finished length of the front boxing strip, measure the seamline from the center front to one side dot and multiply by 2. To determine the finished length of the back boxing strips, measure the seamline from the center back to the same dot and multiply by 2.

Draw a rectangle on paper for the one-piece front boxing cutting pattern: Make the depth the measurement you took from the original cushion boxing (refer to your measuring chart; you used this same measurement when cutting the inside back). Make the length the measurement you took from the cushion template. Draw a ¹/₂" seam allowance on all four sides. Mark the center front on the long edges.

Draw a rectangle on paper for the two-piece back boxing cutting pattern: Make the depth one-half of the boxing depth measurement. Make the length the measurement you took from the dot to the center back. Draw a ¹/₂" seam allowance on all four sides. Mark the center back on the long edges.

Cutting the Inner and Outer Covers

For each cushion needed, you'll cut the inner and outer cover pieces using the cutting patterns you just made. If you're using foam stuffing and polyester padding, you can omit the inner cover.

Cut the outer cover pieces from your upholstery fabric: Cut two pieces using the top/bottom cover cutting pattern. Cut one piece using the front boxing cutting pattern. Cut two pieces using the back boxing cutting pattern. Align or match the fabric pattern on the boxing and cushion top as planned, also match the front boxing to the back boxing (photo 44, page 124).
✂ If your fabric has a wide horizontal repeat, you may have to piece the front boxing strip; place the seam(s) at the cushion corner(s).

Cut the inner cushion pieces from tightly woven ticking or heavy muslin. For each cushion you'll need the same pieces you cut for the outer cover.

putting the cover on the loose cushion

✂If your cover fabric is a solid, or if it has a motif that doesn't require matching, you can chalk-mark the boxing measurements directly on the wrong side of the cover fabric without making paper cutting patterns.

✂If your cushion goes on an open-arm or armless chair, wrap the zipper onto the sides for only 2" and add a pleat to both ends of the front boxing to conceal the zipper ends. When you cut the one-piece boxing strip, add 8" to the length to allow for two 2"-deep pleats.

Sewing the Outside Cover

As an aid in clipping and notching, review Cuts for Fitting, pages 54–56. Refer to Sewing, pages 67–74, for sewing around corners and for joining and finishing the ends of the welting at the back of the cushion. Also see photo 45, page 125.

The welting: With the right sides together and the cut edges aligned, position one end of the welting at the center back edge of the cushion top cover. Machine-baste the welting around the top; clip the seam allowances and pivot at all outside corners; notch as necessary to reduce bulk on inside corners and curves. Stop stitching near the starting point. Lap, trim, and finish the welting ends. Transfer the dots and center marks to the welting seam allowance. ▽

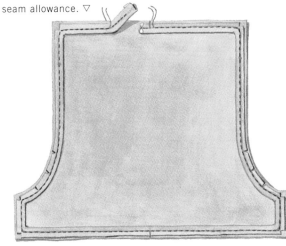

In the same manner, sew welting to the cushion bottom cover.

The front boxing: With the right sides together, sew the front boxing strip to the cushion top cover: Align the end seamlines of the boxing with the dots on the cover sides, and start and stop stitching about 2" from the dots. ▽

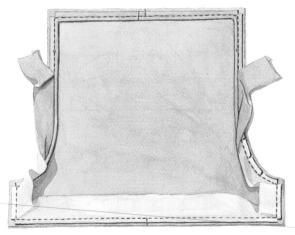

✂If you're making pleats to cover the zipper ends, the boxing should extend beyond the dots; match from the center front out.

✂To match the front boxing strip to the top and bottom pieces, match the center front marks and stitch from corner to corner on the front first.

✂Stitch each area of the cushion separately. Stop and reinforce the seam with a few backstitches at each corner; clip the boxing seam allowances as necessary before stitching the next section. Switch the position of the zipper foot to the other side of the needle as necessary so that all sewing can be done from the same side.

✂Always place welting seams and joined ends in an inconspicuous location. Avoid seams on the front if at all possible.

On the unstitched edge of the boxing, cut a small notch in the seam allowance directly opposite each corner (photo 46, page 125). Later you'll align these notches with corners of the cushion bottom cover. ▷

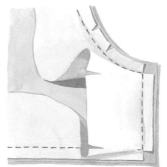

The zipper: Install your zipper foot to the left of the sewing machine needle. Open the zipper and place it right side up so the pull tab is away from you with the left side of the tape under the zipper foot. On one back boxing piece, fold under one long edge and align the fold directly over the edge of the zipper teeth or coil. Topstitch just inside the fold. ▷

Close the zipper and reposition it so the pull tab is away from you. Fold one edge of the second boxing piece in the same manner as for the first. Butt the folds together over the zipper and stitch the second side the same as for the first. ▷

TIPS FROM THE PROS

✂ You can pin the folded edge of each boxing strip to the zipper tape before stitching and then remove the pins as you sew.

✂ If you're sewing a fabric that has a motif, plaid, or stripes, match the pattern along the center folds.

The back boxing: With the right sides together, sew the back boxing strip to the cushion top cover: Align the end seamlines of the boxing with the dots on the cover sides and start and stop stitching about 2" from the dots. Seam together the front and back boxing strips at the dots. Fold the seam allowances toward the front, and finish attaching the boxing to the cover. Notch the boxing opposite the back corners as you did at the front. ▽

✂ If you're concealing the zipper ends, fold the extra fabric at each end of the front boxing into a pleat over the back boxing before attaching the seamed portion to the cover top. ▽

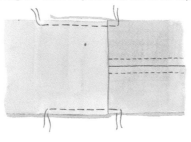

Open the zipper about 3" to provide easy access to the pull tab. Sew the cushion bottom cover to the boxing in one continuous seam, matching corners, centers, and dots. Clip the cover seam allowance on any inward curves. Open the zipper and turn the cover right side out.

putting the cover on the loose cushion

Making a Stuffed Inner Cushion

Sew the inner cushion cover pieces together in the same order as for the outside cover, but omit the welting and zipper. Leave unstitched the opening in the two-piece boxing strip that corresponds to the zipper opening.

Stuff the inner cover with loose polyester stuffing. Using a lock stitch (refer to page 68), sew the opening nearly closed. Pack the cover tightly with more stuffing, and finish closing the opening.

Making a Foam Inner Cushion

To make a foam cushion, you'll need a retractable-blade utility knife or an electric kitchen knife, a can of spray glue to adhere the batting to the large areas of foam, and clear spray foam adhesive to seal the cut edges of the batting along the foam edges.

Cut off the seam allowances from the cover cutting pattern. Pin it to the foam and cut one edge at a time, as shown. ▽

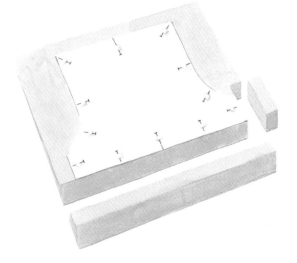

Spray glue onto the bottom face of the foam and place it, glue side down, on a large piece of polyester batting; position it so the batting extends beyond the side and back edges by at least the thickness of the foam, and beyond the front edge by the thickness of the foam plus the front-to-back depth.

Spray glue onto the top face of the foam. Wrap the batting around the front edge onto the top. Trim the batting on the top even with the side and back edges of the foam. Trim the bottom batting so it extends by exactly the thickness of the foam, and trim a square from each back corner. If your cushion is a T-shape, trim the bottom batting even with the bottom edge of the foam along the return of the T, then cut a rectangle of batting to cover the side in this area. ▽

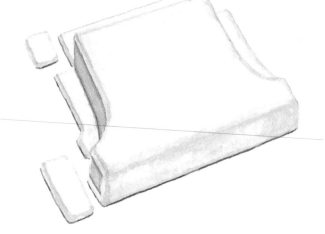

Spray-glue the extending batting to the sides and back of the foam. Spray a line of foam adhesive on the batting edges. Seal the edges by pressing them together with your fingers (photo 47, page 125).

TIPS FROM THE PROS

✂If your batting isn't wide enough to wrap the cushion as described, try to wrap seamlessly around the front, and piece the sides as necessary.

✂When you glue, work in a well-ventilated area and wear latex gloves and a nose/mouth mask.

Assembling the Cushion

With the zipper completely open, insert the T-shape end of the inside cushion into the cover. Arrange the front corners one at a time, and then pull the cover over the rest of the cushion. Close the zipper. Adjust the welting so it lies along the cushion edges.

TIPS FROM THE PROS

✂Don't be surprised—inserting the cushion is awkward. Brace the side or back of the inner cushion against your chest while you pull the cover over it (photo 48, page 125).

THE BORDER AND SKIRT

Although our wing chair provided the opportunity to demonstrate many of the techniques you're likely to use in reupholstery, it has neither a boxing border nor a skirt. Because these are common features on many pieces of furniture, we've included them separately here. Be sure to refer to your stripping notes, as the details of your furniture may be different from those discussed on the following pages.

Marking the Attachment Line

Whether you're installing a border or a skirt, you must first measure and mark the top attachment line on your furniture. You'll need a ruler and some fine nylon string or heavy thread that won't stretch.

✂For a border, measure the depth of the border up from the bottom rail.

✂For a skirt, measure the depth of the skirt up from the floor. Add $1/4$" (the diameter of the welting) to the measurement.

On each corner of the furniture, insert a slip-tack at the measured height into the ditch between the vertical welting and cover edge. If there's no welting, insert it directly through the cover, but be careful not to place it above the desired height.

At a back corner tie the string onto the slip-tack, pull the string tightly along the cover to the next tack, and wrap it around twice. Continue around the frame in this manner until reaching the beginning, and secure the ends by tying them together. ▽

✂If you're installing a border on the front only, place a slip-tack at the front corners only and tie the string to each.

Installing a Front Boxing Border

Install a front boxing border after the seat and other inside sections are completed but before the outside arm is installed. If your border stops at the fascia, as shown in the following illustrations, apply it before installing the fascia; if it extends across the arm front below the fascia, apply the fascia first. Follow the simple steps below to attach the border to the frame.

✂Refer to the next page if you're installing a border all around the furniture.

The welting: With the cord up and the flange down, align the top of the welting under the string. At one end, tack the flange to the arm front. Pull the welting tight across the front of the chair; tack the other end to the other arm front. Working from the center out, permanently tack the welting in place; be sure to keep the top of the cord aligned with the string. Remove the string and slip-tacks.

The border: Use a cardboard tacking strip to blind-tack the top allowance of the boxing strip below the welting. Be sure to center or align any pattern on the fabric appropriately. ▽

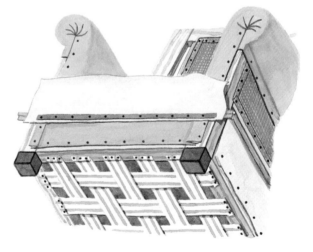

putting on the border and skirt

Position a layer of padding over the area to be covered by the finished boxing strip—from the top of the cardboard strip to the bottom of the rail and up to the inside faces of the arm posts on the sides. ▽

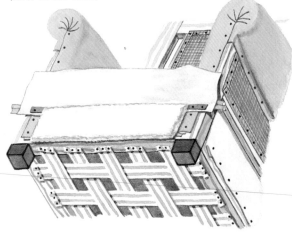

Turn down the boxing over the padding. Stretch and slip-tack it to the bottom face of the front rail, stopping several inches from each leg.

Cut an angled slash through the bottom allowance over the front face of each leg, as shown; aim toward the front inside corner of the leg. Over the front face of each leg, trim the allowance parallel to and about 2" below the top of the leg. ▽

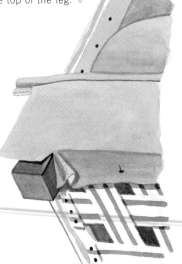

Over the front face of the arm post, turn under the trimmed bottom allowance so the fold aligns with the top of the exposed leg. Stretch and pull the side allowance of the boxing strip outward; permanently tack it to the front face of the arm post. Trim any excess beyond the tacks.

Turn under the remaining edge of the slash, aligning the fold with the inside face of the leg. Permanently tack the bottom allowance to the bottom face of the bottom rail. ▽

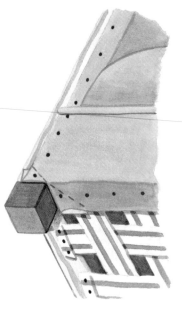

Installing Boxing All Around the Furniture
If the furniture you're reupholstering features boxing on the sides and back as well as the front, install the welting in one piece around the furniture (refer to the skirt instructions, *opposite),* attach the front boxing as explained here, and then attach the side and back boxing as you would a rectangular outside arm and back.

Attaching a Pleated Skirt

Attach a pleated skirt after all the inside and outside upholstery, including the dust cover, is complete. (There's no need to put welting around the bottom of the furniture.) First, sew all the panels and backdrops for the skirt as explained on page 70.

The welting: With the cord up and the flange down, align the top of the welting under the string at the center back. Leaving about 3" free at the end, tack the flange to the frame. Pull the welting tight across the back to the corner; tack to the post. Working from the center out, permanently tack the welting in place; be sure to keep the top of the cord aligned with the string. Pull the welting across the side and tack to the front post, and then tack along the side. Repeat around the furniture; join the welting ends on the back. Remove the string and slip-tacks.

The panels: Mark the junctions of the skirt panels on the front and back (and sides, if applicable) with dressmaker's pins inserted just above the welting.

If there is a center front panel attach it first; otherwise, attach one of the side front panels first. Blind-tack the top edge against the welting with a cardboard tacking strip. Slip-tack first; check to see that the panel hangs properly and that plaid, stripe, or motif lines match the cover as necessary, and then permanently tack. ▽

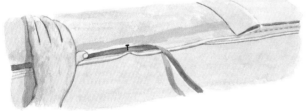

Continue blind-tacking the skirt panels to the furniture in this manner. Attach the side front panels next, then the side panels, then the center back panel if there is one, and the side back panels last.

The backdrops: Holding the skirt panels up, blind-tack the right side of each backdrop against the wrong side of the skirt; center each backdrop over the junction of two panels, including the corners. Omit the tacking strip. ▽

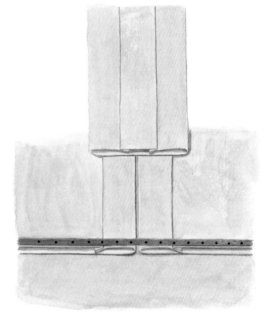

Finishing: Fold down all the skirt and backdrop pieces. Use dressmaker's pins to pin-tack the bottom corners of the skirt pieces to the furniture or to each other, and lightly steam the skirt. Remove the pins. ▽

the process

THERE'S NOTHING LIKE A VIEW OF THE REAL THING to demystify the unfamiliar, so join us as we put a new cover on a traditional wing chair. In this section photographs bring the entire reupholstery process to life. As you look through these pages— whether before or while you redo your own furniture—follow the captions below the photos; they guide you to specific pages in Part Two, where you'll find complete explanations of the actions shown. So unroll your fabric, gather your supplies, and set to work. Don't be surprised, $11^1/_2$ yards of fabric and 5,000 staples later, we have a great looking chair—you should as well.

watching the process unfold

ANALYZING THE OLD COVER

1 Chair before stripping. See pages 20–24 for analyzing; pages 30–31 for making simple drawings and listing cover pieces.

MEASURING

2 Measuring the width of the lip. See page 36 for taking measurements; pages 37–42 for adding allowances, finalizing the dimensions, and calculating the fabric yardage.

CROSS-MARKING

3 Drawing cross-marks between the fascia and inside and outside arms. See page 25 for *cross-marking* definition; page 44 for marking for future reference.

STRIPPING

4 Using a utility knife to cut the stitches holding the old outside back on the chair. See page 43 for the general stripping process and getting started.

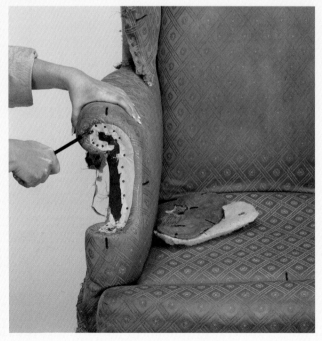

5 Using a claw tool to remove the tacks holding the old inside arm onto the fascia frame. See pages 44–46 for completing the stripping process.

COVERING THE DECK AND LIP

6 Reinforcing the edge of the new burlap on the deck. See page 50 for replacing burlap; page 58 for reinforcing loosely woven edges; page 77 for the wing chair application.

7 Sewing the deck/lip seam allowance to the chair with a running stitch. See page 68 for the running stitch directions; page 80 for attaching the deck/lip cover.

8 Tearing the edge of the new cotton padding on the lip. See page 26 for *padding* definition; page 50 for replacing padding; pages 77 and 80 for the wing chair application.

10 A straight slash has been cut on the deck, behind the vertical scroll post; the lip has been slashed around the post. See page 54 for slash basics; page 81 for fitting the deck/lip.

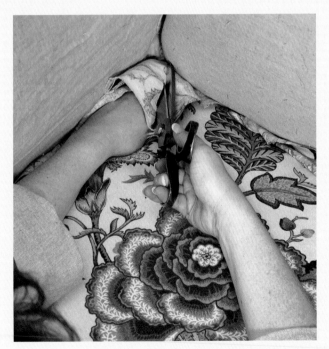

9 Making the diagonal cut at the back corner of the deck. See page 55 for diagonal corner cut basics; page 80 for fitting the deck and lip; page 83 for fitting a tight seat.

11 Slip-tacking the front edge of the lip cover to the bottom of the front rail. See page 27 for *slip-tacking* definition; page 57 for securing fabrics temporarily.

12 Adding polyester padding to the inside arm and securing it to the fascia; the excess padding on the right arm has been trimmed. See pages 50 and 77 for basic how-tos; page 84 for covering the inside arm.

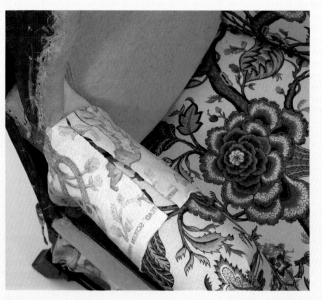

14 A Y-cut slash has been made on the inside arm along the top of the horizontal arm scroll to allow the inside arm to fit around the wing. See page 55 for how to make a Y-cut-slash; page 86 for covering the inside arm.

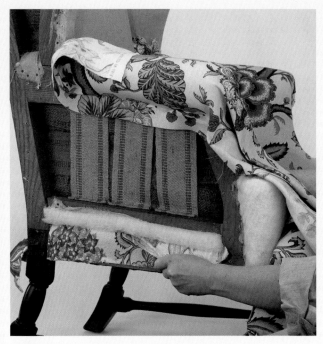

13 Pulling the inside arm bottom allowance to the outside, under the arm liner, through the crevice between the arm and deck. See page 87 for covering the inside arm.

15 Stretching and tacking the top inside arm allowance to the outside of the frame, under the horizontal scroll. See page 88 for covering the inside arm.

watching the process unfold

THE FASCIA AREA

16 Slashing the inside arm bottom allowance so you can fit it around the vertical scroll post. See pages 54–56 for slashing basics; pages 86–87 for covering the inside arm.

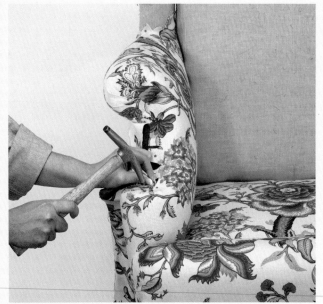

18 Pleating and slip-tacking the inside arm to the fascia frame. See pages 84–93 for the various ways to attach an inside arm and fascia to one another and to the furniture.

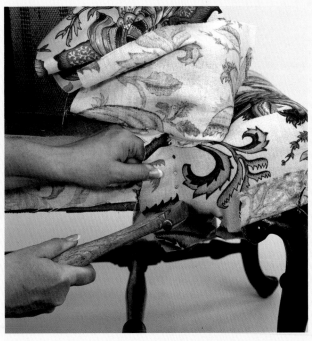

17 Stretching and tacking the lip behind the vertical scroll post. Note how the bottom allowance is turned up over the leg. See pages 82 and 87 for finishing the lip.

19 Using the old fascia cover as a cutting pattern for the new fascia. See pages 51–52 for cutting pieces that will be sewn together.

20 Sewing welting to the fascia, clipping the flange around the curve. See pages 51 and 72–74 for cutting and sewing welting.

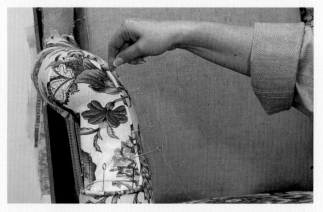

21 Sewing the pin-tacked fascia to the inside arm. See page 68 for blindstitching; page 89 for attaching the fascia to the wing chair.

22 Tacking the welting to the outside arm along the edge of the fascia. See page 90 for finishing the wing chair fascia.

THE INSIDE WING

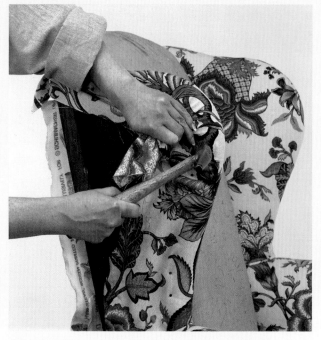

23 Slip-tacking the back allowance of the inside wing to the back post. See page 89.

24 Stretching and slip-tacking the top/front allowance of the inside wing to the outside face of the frame. See page 62 for stretching basics; page 89 for attaching the inside wing.

THE INSIDE BACK

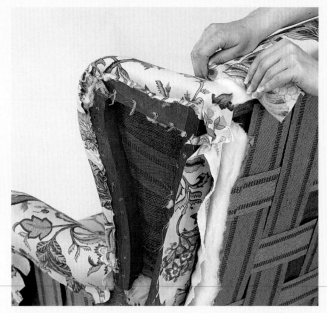

25 Slip-tacking the top allowance of the inside back to the outside face of the top rail, working from the center out to each side. See page 94.

27 Folding under the side allowance above the slash made in the previous photo. Turn to page 95 to see the finished top allowance on the inside back.

26 Using your fingers to locate the top rail and slashing the side allowance of the inside back so it can be pulled through to the outside. See page 94.

28 Trimming the inside wing and inside back side allowances parallel to the back post. See page 95 for permanently tacking and trimming these allowances.

THE OUTSIDE WING

29 Tacking welting along the outside face of the wing frame. See page 98.

31 Partially closing the flexible tacking strip jaw. See pages 60–61 for flexible tacking strip basics.

30 Guiding and tacking the flexible tacking strip over the welting on the outside wing. See pages 60–61 for flexible strip basics; page 98 for attaching it to the outside arm and wing.

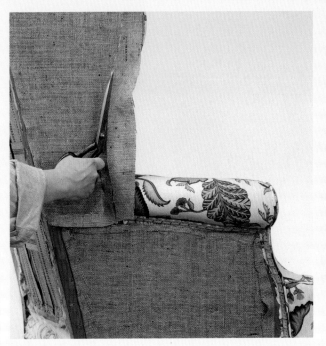

32 Trimming the new burlap on the outside wing. See page 50 for replacing burlap; page 58 for reinforcing loosely woven edges; pages 77 and 98 for the wing chair application.

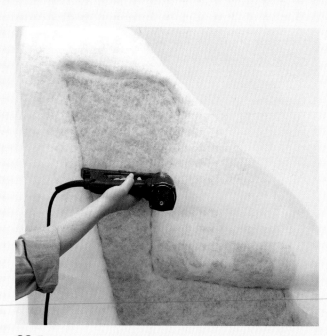

33 Tacking a large sheet of polyester padding to the outside arm/outside wing. See pages 50 and 77 for basic how-tos; page 99 for attaching padding to the outside arm/outside wing.

35 Tucking the outside arm/outside wing allowance into the flexible strip jaw with a regulator. See pages 60–61 for flexible strip basics; page 99 for covering the outside arm/outside wing.

34 Pin-tacking the outside arm/outside wing cover into the flexible tacking strip jaw. See page 26 for definition of *pin-tacking;* page 99 for covering the outside arm/outside wing.

36 Trimming the allowance of the outside wing after it's been tucked into the flexible strip jaw. See page 61 for flexible strip basics; page 99 for finishing the outside arm/outside wing.

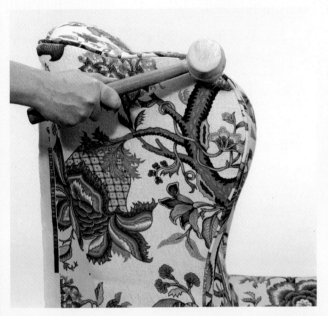

37 Using a mallet to close the flexible strip, thus securing and concealing the edge of the outside wing. See page 61 for basics; page 99 for finishing the outside arm/outside wing.

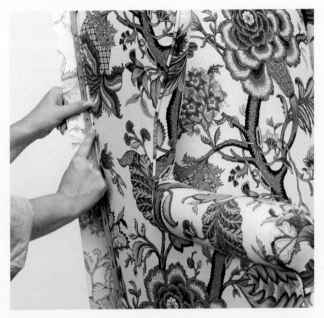

39 Pressing the side allowance of the outside back onto the teeth of a rigid metal tacking strip. See page 59 for rigid metal tacking strip basics; page 101 for covering the outside back.

38 Folding under the slashed bottom allowance of the outside arm above the back leg. See page 54 for slashing basics; page 100 for finishing the outside arm/outside wing.

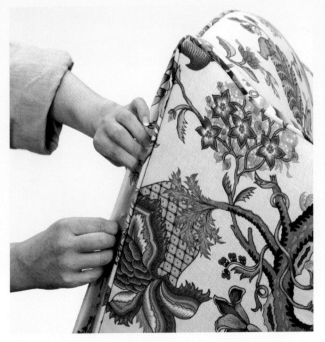

40 Turning the rigid metal tacking strip over, positioning the teeth for insertion in the back post. See page 59 for rigid metal tacking strip basics; page 101 for finishing the outside back.

ATTACHING WELTING TO THE BOTTOM RAILS

41 Gluing trimmed welting around the back leg. Some furniture has a groove above the leg to hold the welting flange. See page 102 for adding welting to the bottom rail.

THE DUST COVER

42 A view of the dust cover, which completely conceals the webbing and the cut edges on the bottom rail. See page 103.

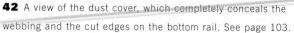

THE CUSHION

43 A piece of cambric shaped and chalk-marked for a cushion cover cutting pattern. Dressmaker's pins hold the slashed fabric out of the way. See page 104.

44 Matching the pattern on the cushion boxing prior to sewing. See pages 69–70 for machine sewing.

45 Joining the welting ends as you sew the welting to the cushion top. See page 74 for joining welting ends.

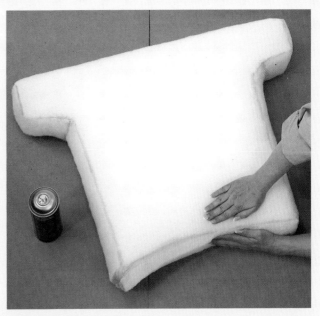

47 Gluing padding over the foam cushion form. See page 108 for making inside cushions.

46 Notching the corner alignment on the cushion cover boxing. See pages 106–107 for sewing a loose cushion cover.

48 Bracing the inner cushion while pulling the cushion cover over it. See page 108.

THE FINISHED CHAIR

49 On the back, the dominant floral motif appears comfortably balanced; note how it is centered horizontally but placed a bit high. On the side, it's centered under the arm.

50 Good planning pays off—the pattern matches perfectly from lip to cushion to inside back. Look closely and you'll see that this wide horizontal repeat was pieced at the lip corner.

index

index